Swimming wit...

George Huang began his Hollywood career in San Francisco as an intern for Lucasfilm. After working as an assistant for Paramount Pictures, Universal, Warner Brothers, Disney and Columbia, he turned his experiences into his writing/directing debut, *Swimming with Sharks*, which won the critics award at the Deauville Film Festival and several acting awards from the Independent Spirit Awards and the New York Film Critics Circle. Since then, he has worked on the films *Trojan War*, *S.W.A.T.*, *The Faculty* and *Spy Kids*. A graduate of UC Berkeley and the USC School of Cinema-Television, he currently resides in Manhattan Beach, California… just outside of Hollywood.

Michael Lesslie, born in 1983 and currently living in London, wrote and directed *A Triple Bill of Shame* for Hip Street Productions which had an acclaimed run at the 2003 Edinburgh Fringe Festival. In 2005 his adaptation of *The Constant Prince* had an international tour and transferred to London's Arcola Studio and the Oxford Playhouse. The same year his play *Face Up, Face Down* was awarded the Cameron Mackintosh Award for New Writing by Patrick Marber, under whose guidance the script has subsequently been developed. He has recently completed a feature film adaptation of Brian Moore's Booker Prize-nominated novel *Lies of Silence*, and written a number of short films, including the BAFTA-nominated and Smirnoff Reel Talent Award-winning *Heavy Metal Drummer* (which he co-wrote) and *Airlock, or How to Say Goodbye in Space*, which premiered at the 2007 Edinburgh Film Festival.

George Huang

Swimming with Sharks

in a version by
Michael Lesslie

Methuen Drama

Published by Methuen Drama 2007

1 3 5 7 9 10 8 6 4 2

Methuen Drama
A & C Black Publishers Limited
38 Soho Square
London W1D 3QZ
www.acblack.com

ISBN: 978 1 408 10406 4

A CIP catalogue record for this book
is available from the British Library

Typeset by Country Setting, Kingsdown, Kent
Printed and bound in Great Britain by
Bookmarque Ltd, Croydon, Surrey

Swimming with Sharks in a version by Michael Lesslie was commissioned by Creative Management and Productions Limited. The production premiered at the Vaudeville Theatre, London, on 5 October 2007 and was produced by Creative Management and Productions Limited, Nica Burns, Max Weitzenhoffer for Nimax Theatres, The Weinstein Company, Old Vic Productions, Ian Lenagan and Ian Osborne. The cast was as follows:

Rex	Arthur Darvill
Guy	Matt Smith
Buddy Ackerman	Christian Slater
Mitzy	Elizabeth Croft
Dawn Lockard	Helen Baxendale
Cyrus Miles	Jonathan Newth
Daniel Faruk	Fanos Xenofos
Jack	Mark Edel-Hunt

Director   Wilson Milam
Designer   Dick Bird
Lighting Designer   Paul Anderson
Composer   Stephen Warbeck
Sound Designer   Matt McKenzie for Autograph

Swimming with Sharks

Characters

Rex, *Buddy's old assistant*
Guy, *Buddy's new assistant*
Buddy Ackerman, *Co-Senior Executive Vice President of Production for Keystone Productions*
Mitzy, *an aspiring model-cum-actress*
Dawn Lockard, *an independent producer working for Premium Productions on the Keystone lot*
Cyrus Miles, *the founder and Chairman of Keystone Productions*
Daniel Faruk, *a fledgling movie director*
Jack, *a film-school friend of Guy's*

The cleaner in Scene Two can be played either by an understudy or by the one of the actors playing Mitzy, Daniel or Jack.
A barman to deliver Guy's drink in Scene Three is optional.

Time

Present day.

Location

Hollywood, Los Angeles: the offices of Keystone Productions, a major film production company; a bar; Dawn's apartment; Buddy's apartment.

Stage Directions

The descriptions of soundscapes are suggestions only. The exact qualities of the pieces used are left to the discretion of the director and producers.

The playscript that follows was correct at the time of going to press, but may have changed during rehearsals.

Act One

Scene One

Keystone. The stage comprises the large antechamber of **Buddy Ackerman**'s *office and the office itself.*

Facing the main entrance of the antechamber is a meticulous desk bearing a phone and a computer. Opposite the desk is a sleek sofa. A door leads to a kitchenette closet, unseen. The walls of the antechamber seem to be made of scripts and novel manuscripts, bound stacks of white paper differentiated only by the titles printed on their spines in thick black marker pen.

Two huge, clear-glass doors separate **Buddy**'s *office from the antechamber. They read 'Keystone Pictures' in plain, bold, frosted lettering and, beneath this in slightly smaller frosted lettering, 'Buddy Ackerman'.*

Buddy's *office can be seen through the clear-glass doors. It is furnished in a minimalist, masculine manner, the decor dominated by an imposing desk and a wheeling desk chair. A phone sits on the desk. A door leads to an executive bathroom, unseen. Shelves of awards run along the wall, glittering in the distance.*

Rex *sits at the antechamber's desk in a wheeling desk chair, phone receiver cradled in his neck, writing on a script. He wears a slick shirt.*

Rex (*into phone*)   Derek, listen, he may very well be due in a meeting with Stella, but he's in another meeting right now and can only be with you two steps ahead of humanly possible. (*Beat.*) The other side of town, not that it's any of your fuckin' business. Hold the line. (*He hits a button on the phone.*) Buddy Ackerman's office. (*Beat.*) I'm sorry, he's out of the country right now, but I'll be sure to – (*Beat.*) Minsk. (*He hits a button on the phone.*) Derek, with you in a minute. (*He hits a button on the phone.*) Rob? Great, now, you say you want to lower the volume on the sound mix, and I just thought I oughta check, 'cause Buddy got in early this morning and he looks pissed.

Guy *enters the antechamber, nervous in his first suit.* **Rex** *glances up at him.*

Rex (*into phone*)   I'm lookin' at him right now, Rob. Triple-pissed, red-faced, and breathin' fire, so I think you oughta be sure that the person askin' you to face that is worth your nine last lives. Who was it? (*Beat.*) You can't say? Hold the line. (*He hits a button on the phone.*) Derek, that was Buddy, he's just left the meeting, he'll be with you quicker than conscious thought, I promise. (*Beat.*) What do you care who he's meeting? Last time I checked, Derek, Stella was your concern, Buddy was mine, and I wasn't in the mood for a goddamn transplant. PS, you know a good dry-cleaner's? Buddy had the last deported and I need his tux steamed by yesterday. (*Beat.*) I love you, Derek. Hold the line. (*He hits a button on the phone.*) Rob, I just told Buddy about the sound mix, it doesn't look good.

Rex *calmly holds the phone receiver away from his mouth.*

Guy   Hi, I –

Rex   FUCK YOU.

Guy   Excuse me?

Rex (*into phone*)   Yes, that was him, Rob, and as you can hear, he's a little put out by the news, so you better tell me who gave the order and I'll do what I can to smooth it over. (*Beat.*) Stella? It was Stella? Thank you, Rob. Hold the line. (*He bangs a button on the phone.*) You cheating piece of shit, Derek, you carried the call on the fuckin' sound mix? (*Beat.*) Screw you, my friend, you're wrong, this is about loyalty, loyalty to what matters most, me, and I'll ask you to remember that when you're starin' up at the skyline of my new office. (*Beat.*) Mmm-hmm. Gonna miss you too, Derek.

He pushes hold, and then presses and holds the hang-up button on the phone set. The receiver stays cradled in his neck. He swivels in his chair, still holding down the button, and looks at **Guy**.

Rex   Beautiful day.

Guy   I'm Guy, I'm –

Rex   Yes, you are. How was the flight?

Guy   Actually, it –

The phone rings. Before the first ring is completed, **Rex** *lets go of the hang-up button.*

Rex (*into phone*)   Buddy Ackerman's office. (*Beat.*) Well, hello, Mrs Ackerman, and how are you today? (*Beat.*) I'm very sorry to hear that, because Buddy's in a meeting right now. Could you – (*Beat.*) That's it, Mrs Ackerman. Holding you now.

Rex *pushes hold, and then pushes and holds the hang-up button again.*

Guy   His wife?

Rex   God, no. His mother.

Guy   Oh.

Rex   Lady wife's long gone. Other side a' the fuckin' world, all we know. Trust me, you don't wanna join her, don't mention it.

Guy   OK.

Rex   To anyone.

Guy   OK.

Rex   The flight was what?

Guy   What? Oh – it was –

Rex   What?

Guy   Nonexistent, actually. I drove in yesterday, so –

The phone rings. Before the first ring is completed, **Rex** *lets go of the hang-up button.*

Rex (*into phone*)   Buddy Ackerman's off . . . course I recognize you, Mona baby, angel choirs don't sing more clear. (*Beat.*) I know what he said, but Buddy's a busy man. (*Beat.*) I'll tell you what you do. You fix yourself a smile and get your cute little butt over to his place by midnight. (*Beat.*) All right then. The key'll be – (*Beat.*) You got it. Bye, beautiful.

He hangs up the phone receiver.

Guy   Busy line.

Rex   Lines. Many of them.

Guy   OK.

Rex   Because Buddy is a busy man.

Guy   Yes.

Rex   Which means you, my friend, are about to become a very, very busy man. (*Beat.*) Nice suit.

Guy   Thank you. It's – uh – it's new.

Rex   I don't know what you've heard about this job.

Guy   Well, I know it's the most prestigious –

Rex   That is correct.

Guy   And it's the top position I could, well, realistically be hoping for at –

Rex   It's gonna be a lot of work for shit wages. A lot of shit work for shit wages. Picking up dry-cleaning, gassing his car, getting him coffee, getting him lunch, getting him laid. And he can be, well – difficult at times. But such are the demands of greatness. Buddy Ackerman is, after all, the Senior Executive Vice President here at Keystone, Guy, third rung in the whole company. Numero Three.

Guy   Equal.

Rex   I beg your pardon?

Guy   Isn't he – I read that Stella Smiley –

Rex   Whoa, careful with that name.

Guy   What?

Rex   Not in here. Stella Smiley is the enemy. The competition.

Guy   But I read – she works for Keystone too.

Rex   That may be so, my friend, but in a different division, therefore a different country, and one with which we are at war. Worldwide Production. The independents, the foreign languages, the nurturing of newborn talent. Fucking romcoms. These are not our business, Guy. These belong to the softer sex. Stella Smiley? Spit the name. But you've done your homework. That's good. Yes, Buddy is, technically, Co-Senior Exec VP.

Guy   That's what I thought.

Rex   For now. Changes are being rung.

Guy   Really?

Rex   Take my word.

Guy   How do you know?

Rex   Collective waters. Spend your time here, you sense these things. Your mind, your instinct, is no longer your own. It belongs to the office. To the team. To Buddy.

Guy   'Thoughtcrime is death.'

Rex   What?

Guy   *Nineteen Eighty-Four*.

Rex   An intellectual.

Guy   I saw the movie.

Rex   Well, don't worry. Execution ain't in the small print.

Guy   No.

Rex   For now. But as I say, changes are being rung. You've arrived at the right time, Guy. Between yourself and mine, Number Two is out.

Guy   Matthew McCoy?

Rex   President of Production is soon to be vacated, take my word.

Guy   He got fired?

Rex   He got cancer.

Guy Jesus.

Rex I know. We're all devastated. (*Beat.*) But he's out.

Guy And Buddy's in.

Rex It's a matter of time. Buddy's slate of horrorporn broke Keystone records. And that's after his mid-nineties action spree. Lookit. Three of his six October releases came in under five mil –

Guy Under five? That's incredible.

Rex And all broke fifteen on opening weekend. It's a question of figures. *Grind* cost one point two, opened at eighteen point three. Took fifty-five point two million in the US alone. *Grind Two*? Cost four, opened at thirty-one point seven, has now taken one hundred and fifty-two million US dollars worldwide.

Guy Jesus.

Rex *Three*'s budgeted at twelve. You do the math. The *Meat Machine* franchise, the remake frenzy, sequels, trilogies – one man. Buddy. He's brought exploitation into the mainstream and the floodgates have opened. Giving the people what they want, my friend, and lots of it – fuck purpose, cover the lens in blood. Way I see it, the board doesn't have a choice. It's as good as his.

Guy What about –

Rex Stella?

Guy Yeah.

Rex A woman.

Guy So?

Rex So the world outside may be crumbling into equality, rookie, but in here we stick to what works.

Guy I heard she was terrifying.

Rex   Don't be fooled. She may clothe her bulldog body in the trousered suits of power, Guy, and she may roar and rage with the best of our kind, ruthless cougar as she is, but believe me, inside, she has the melting taste of a Lancôme fag cryin' lonely over shell-shape soap. And that, my friend, is why Stella Smiley ain't the smart bet for President of Production. Not if you ask me. Because above us all, Numero Uno, is Cyrus Miles, studio chairman and grand Pooh-Bah. Likes his movies tough and his men male. We call him God.

Guy   Is he here?

Rex   Lake Como, half the year. Rest of it, on our asses.

Guy   Como, huh?

Rex   Guy, if you do this job well, wealth and opportunity are yours, and fast. All of Buddy's assistants have gone on to bigger and better things in two, three years, maximum. One is running the Sony Channel. Another has all rights to the Kota Fanning action franchise.

Guy   But –

Rex   What?

Guy   Dakota Fanning's thirteen.

Rex   And opens a movie at twenty-five mil.

Guy   Wow.

Rex   The Ackerman assistant is a good lineage.

Guy   Where are you going?

Rex   VP of Production at Paramount. Like I said, it is a good lineage.

Guy   Sounds like a movie.

Rex   What does?

Guy   The Ackerman Assistant. Like a – an *Odessa File*. Or an *Idaho Kid*.

Rex   A film buff, I see.

Guy   Of course. Why else would I be here?

Rex   Money, girls, and power.

Guy   OK.

Rex   Never work in what you love, rookie.

Guy   Why not?

Rex   Because it becomes work. This – this is not the movies. This is the business of the movies. You'll do well to separate the two. (*Beat.*) You sure you're in the right place? You're gonna stick this, you gotta be ready to crush anyone and anything that comes within a mile of getting in your way, and that without a second, without a snap of thought. Are you ready for that?

Guy   I just want to make movies.

Rex   All right then. To work. (*Indicating the phone.*) This, my friend, is going to be the single most important item in your entire life. Forty lines, all of them hot, all of them flowin' through this one piece of plastic.

Guy   OK.

Rex (*gesturing to the kitchenette*)   Second most important lives in there.

Guy   What is it?

Rex   Coffee machine.

Guy   I don't drink coffee.

Rex   What?

Guy   Messes with my stomach.

Rex   What do you drink?

Guy   I don't know. Smoothies?

Rex   Not anymore. Buddy hates health. Say it with me.
I drink coffee.

Guy   I drink coffee.

Rex   I love coffee.

Guy   I love coffee.

Rex   Don't worry, rookie. You'll do all right.

Guy   Actually, ah, I graduated a year ago now.

Buddy *enters. Easy in his power but energized by ambition and watchful, with a smile that breaks backs.* **Guy** *doesn't notice him. The phone rings.* **Rex** *answers.* **Buddy** *approaches predatorily.*

Rex (*into phone*)   Buddy Ackerman's office.

Guy   I'm actually quite experienced, for my age. I mean, I've made a couple of shorts already, and –

Buddy   You must be Guy.

Guy *spins round, terrified.*

Guy   Hello.

Buddy   I like that. 'Guy'. It's anonymous. (*Offering his hand.*)
Buddy Ackerman.

Guy (*shaking* **Buddy**'*s hand*)   Thank you, it's great to –

Buddy   So glad to see you here. I cannot tell you how grateful I am that you could start right away. It'll be nice to finally get some real help around here, get rid of this mongoloid so he'll stop screwing me up and fuck the competition for a change, huh? Our gain is their loss. (*To* **Rex**.) What?

Rex   Stella meet's line one, Mom's on two, and they called from the stage, they want us to lower the volume on the final mix.

Buddy   Who's they?

Rex   Rob called you, Stella called him.

Buddy Stella? No fuckin' wonder.

Rex Called in person.

Buddy That's not a person, Rex, that's a knife with hips.
Get me Rob on the phone.

Rex He's on three.

Buddy I'll take him, tell the Stella meet to hold, take my
mom, and when you're done with her, west lobby, tank top,
ankle boots, hurry, fetch. Come on, Guy, you're in for a treat.

Rex *punches a button on the phone.*

Rex *(into phone)* Derek, he'll be right down.

Buddy Nice suit, by the way.

Guy Thank you, it's —

Rex Rob is ready.

Buddy Throw him through.

Buddy and **Guy** *enter* **Buddy**'s *office.* **Buddy** *moves to his desk
and puts on a phone headset.* **Rex** *puts the call through and then pushes
a button for another line.*

Rex *(into phone)* West lobby, please.

Buddy *(into phone)* Yo, Rob, how's Chrissie? *(Beat.)* Still? Must
be tough on the kids. Listen, I ran the rough cut last night and
the mix is still way too goddamn low. I told you you gotta
bring up the screaming, you gotta be loud loud loud, the
audience should feel their balls tremble, their ears should
bleed. So I don't care if God told you to keep it down, much
less Stella. *(Beat. He mouths to* **Guy***: 'Sit sit sit.')*

Guy *does so.*

Buddy *(into phone)* Hey, what do you mean, can't be done, *que
pasa* this can't be done? *(Beat.)* All right, Rob, shut up for a
second. Let's try something easier. Repeat this. 'Would you like

that in a pump or a loafer?' (*Beat.*) No, Rob, just say it with me, come on, just humor me, just say it once, just . . . 'Would you like that in a pump or a loafer?' (*Beat.*) Good, now memorize it, because as of tomorrow the only job you're going to be able to get is selling shoes.

Buddy *hangs up. Pause.* **Buddy** *picks up and sets in motion a wind-up toy on his desk.*

Guy   Well, I, uh –

Buddy   Shh shh shh.

They watch the walking windup toy. Pause. **Rex**'s *phone rings.* **Rex** *answers.*

Rex (*into phone*)   Buddy Ack— (*Calling.*) Rob's calling again on line one.

Buddy *feigns surprise and presses a button on the phone.*

Buddy (*into phone*)   Yo, Rob, look, I'm busy now, I can't really – (*Beat.*) Well, I'm glad you see it my way. Now. (*Beat.*) Hey, look, we all have our misunderstandings, just get it done. (*He hangs up. Shouting to* **Rex**.) Where's Stella and what's my schedule?

Rex *jogs into the office.*

Rex   They hung up. She wants you down there right away.

Buddy   They start yet?

Rex   No, you're co-chairing. She's been waiting for you for about fifteen minutes.

Buddy   Good. Let me tell you something, Guy, and learn from this. If they can't start a meeting without you, well, that's a meeting worth going to, isn't it? And that's the only kind of meeting you should ever concern yourselves with. (*He picks a folder up off his desk and throws it at* **Rex**.) File this. What's next?

Rex   Her name is Mitzy.

Buddy   I like that.

Rex *jogs out of the office and offstage.* **Buddy** *exits to his executive bathroom for a few seconds and then reenters, smooth* **Rex** *shows* **Mitzy** *into the office. Numerically gorgeous, dressed as available.*

Buddy You must be Mitzy. Hi. Buddy Ackerman, Senior Exec VP of Production. VP means Vice President, I'm sorry.

Mitzy (*clear, clean little Valley Girl voice*) I –

Buddy I couldn't help it, but I saw you in the lobby on my way in and – I'm on my way to a very important meeting and I can just tell that there are enormous opportunities for the both of us, and I will pull myself out of this meeting, if you can bear just waiting ten minutes, because I would love it if you and I could just . . . sit and chat.

Mitzy *giggles.*

Buddy Would that be possible?

Mitzy Sure, I guess.

Buddy Oh, that's great. That's just wonderful. Now, if you need anything, you just ask these two boys here, OK? (*To* **Rex**.) Keep her happy, all right? (*To* **Mitzy**.) So, why don't you just go sit down? And I'll be right back.

Buddy *pushes a button as he leaves his office, frosting the windows. He slams the door.*

Buddy Where's my fucking coffee?

The phone rings.

Rex Rookie, first job.

Guy *runs to the kitchenette.* **Rex** *picks up the phone.*

Rex (*into phone*) Buddy Ackerman's off— (*Beat.*) Mr Miles. Yes, sir, no trouble at all, he's right here. (*To* **Buddy**.) It's Cyrus.

Buddy *immediately heads to his office and picks up the phone. As he talks he evicts* **Mitzy** *to the antechamber.*

Buddy (*into phone*)   Cap'n Miles. How in the hell are you, sir? (*Beat.*) Good to hear it. You better catch one for me, Cap'n, fish over here's older than I am. What can I do you for?

Buddy *closes the door of his office.* **Dawn** *enters and stands in the main entrance: beautiful, poised, furious.*

Dawn   Who drives a red-tin piece of shit, New York plates 233 ass?

Another phone line rings. **Rex** *picks up.*

Rex (*into phone*)   Buddy Ackerman's office.

Dawn   Who drives a red-tin piece of shit, New York plates 233 ass?

Rex (*into phone*)   He left already, Derek, he'll be there before you can hang up the phone.

Dawn   Somebody better fuckin' answer me or I'll be nailing wrists to trees. Who drives a red-tin piece of shit, New York plates 233 ass?

Guy *appears from the closet.*

Guy   Oh, Jesus, that's me.

Dawn   I knew it'd be this office.

Guy   AS5.

Dawn   What?

Guy   233 AS5. Not ass. My name's Guy, by the way.

Dawn   I'm Toto.

Guy   Hi, how are you?

Dawn   Fuck you, you're in my spot. Could you move?

Guy   OK, sure, sorry. I didn't realize that was your spot.

Dawn   You can see it from the building. It's a producer's. It's mine. I earned it.

Guy It's a great spot. Soon as I pulled in I thought, wow, what a great spot.

Dawn Now.

Guy Sure, I'll – soon as I'm done here, I'll –

Dawn What is this, your first day on the job or something?

Guy Yes, yes, as a matter of fact it is.

Dawn Yeah, well, piece of advice, lose the smile, makes you look like a schmuck. Fuckin' interns.

Guy Acutally, I'm –

Dawn Where'd you find this one, Rex, Democrat pre-school?

The phone rings. **Rex** *answers immediately.*

Rex (*into phone*) Buddy Ackerman's office.

Dawn Nice suit, by the way.

Guy *looks down at his suit.* **Dawn** *leaves.*

Guy Thanks, it's – (*Looking back up.*) G'bye now. (*Beat.*) Christ.

Guy *runs back into the kitchenette.* **Buddy** *bursts out of his office, jubilant.*

Buddy Inoperable.

Rex What?

Buddy McCoy's a goner. He's lost a lung.

Rex Congratulations.

Buddy Meeting set up, soon as the Pooh-Bah's back from Como. President of Production, Rex. I can taste it. I can feel it. I can see it jamming down Stella's fucking throat. Yes. Right. Now. Where am I?

Rex Co-chairing, Stella, five minutes ago.

Buddy *looks down at his empty hands.*

Buddy Where's my fucking coffee?

Guy *runs out of the kitchenette and places a cup of coffee, a container of cream and a sachet of sugar on the desk in front of* **Buddy**.

Guy   Cream, sugar.

Buddy   Sweet'N Low.

Guy *runs back to the coffee machine.* **Buddy** *and* **Rex** *exchange a cynical glance.*

Buddy   Come on, people, I'm late for a meeting here, let's go go go go go.

Guy *arrives back with sweetener and gives it to* **Buddy**. **Buddy** *looks at the packet, pauses, and holds it up.*

Buddy   Excuse me, what is this?

Guy   Sweet'N Low?

Buddy   No. This is not Sweet'N Low, this is Equal. Blue packet. Sweet'N Low is pink, see? Equal blue, Sweet'N Low pink. It's not the same thing, is it?

Guy   Uh, well, I think they both contain the same am–

Buddy   What Equal contains is not my concern here. I don't care if it has fucking fairy dust in it. What I am concerned with is detail. I asked you to go get me a packet of Sweet'N Low, you bring me back Equal. That isn't what I asked for, that isn't what I wanted, that isn't what I needed, and that shit isn't going to work around here.

Guy   I just thought that –

Buddy   You thought. Do me a fucking favor. Shut up, listen, and learn. Look, I know that this is your first day and you don't really know how things work around here –

Guy   No –

Buddy   So I will tell you. You have no brain. No judgment calls are necessary. What you think means nothing. What you feel means nothing. You are here for me. You are here to protect my interests and to serve my needs. So, while it may look like a little thing to you, when I ask for a packet of Sweet'N Low, that's what I want. And it is your responsibility now to see that I get what I want. Am I clear?

Guy   Yes, sir.

Buddy   Good. I'm not trying to be cruel, I'm just trying to help, because, if you do this job right, if you listen and learn, then you're going to be able to do anything you want in this town.

Guy   OK.

Buddy   You can have whatever you want. We're on the up. I mean, Christ, look at Rex here. A VP at Paramount. Hah! Rex. What a name. Belongs to a fuckin' mutt. So look, Guy, if I can get this mongrel a job, you – you might just do OK.

Buddy *leaves with his coffee.* **Guy** *slumps in the waiting chair.*

Guy   I fucked up. It's over.

Rex   Relax. He does that a lot. Tomorrow he'll ask you for an Equal. It's a lose–lose situation.

Guy   Does it still happen to you?

Rex   Daily. Actually hourly. Look, what he wants, what he needs, can change in a second. The trick is to have everything ready. Anticipate. Next time bring back an Equal and a Sweet'N Low. Remember, protect his interests and serve his needs. Come on, say it with me. 'Protect his interests and serve his needs.'

Guy   Protect his interests and serve his needs, OK, but that's crazy, that's no way to run a business.

Rex   Uh-uh. First mistake. This is not a business. No rules here. Save that candy-striped crap for the Wall Street wimps. This is show business. Punching below the belt is not only all right, it is rewarded. So in this – this business of show – you got to ask yourself, what is it that's going to make them sit up and take notice of you?

Guy   Work really, really hard.

Rex   Don't worry, rookie. You'll learn.

Mitzy *opens the door of* **Buddy***'s office.*

Mitzy (*harsh*)   I want a coffee.

Guy   Jesus.

Rex   I beg your pardon?

Mitzy   I said, I want a coffee.

Rex   Machine's over there.

Mitzy   Your boss said –

Rex   My boss said you had enormous opportunities, princess, but I don't see anything near that size. So. If you want to keep your meeting, you listen to me. Get back in there, get under his desk, and wait quietly like a good little girl.

Mitzy *hesitates, and then storms back into the office, slamming the doors.*

Guy   Her voice.

Rex   Just be thankful he doesn't like boys. Come on. Roll up your sleeves, rookie. We got some training to do.

Scene Two

Keystone, nine weeks later. **Guy** *is on the phone, sitting at his desk. He wears slicker clothes. His back is to the main entrance, the phone receiver to his ear.*

Guy (*into phone*)   I'm sorry, Derek, I'll do what I can, but I – (*Beat.*) I'll try, but –

Dawn *enters and approaches the desk.*

Dawn   Hi, I'm Dawn Lockard, I'm a producer on the lot for Premium, I'm here to see –

Guy *swivels round in his chair.* **Dawn** *recognizes him.*

Dawn   To see Buddy. (*Beat.*) Hi.

Guy (*ignoring the phone*)   Hi.

Dawn   You lost the suit.

Guy   Yeah, well. All the compliments started to get to me.

Dawn *smiles.*

Guy   Buddy's running a little late, so just, uh, have a seat.

Dawn *sits in the waiting chair. She starts to apply lipstick.* **Guy** *stares. She notices* **Guy** *staring and smiles.*

Guy (*into phone*)   Uh, yes, fine, I'll tell him.

Guy *hangs up the phone. It immediately starts to ring again. He ignores it. Beat.*

Dawn   Listen. About that parking spot thing. I thought you were a temp or something. Had I known you were Buddy's new assistant, I certainly would have let you –

Guy   Don't worry about it, really.

Dawn   No, I'm just saying, you get enough shit from him, you don't need it from me.

Guy   Believe me, I can handle Buddy.

Buddy *enters furiously and hurls a script at* **Guy**.

Buddy   Pick up the phone pick up the phone pick up pick up pick up. Don't you have hands?

Guy   I'm sorry, the lines've been going crazy.

Buddy   I don't care. If I get that answering machine one more time I draw blood. Where's Stella?

Guy   Uh, just spoke to her office, she's not going to be back till Wednesday.

Buddy   What do you mean, not back?

Guy   Well, evidently she's white-water rafting in Colorado with Tom Cruise.

Buddy   Cruise? Hah! She is desperate. Track her down, get her on the phone. We're going to fuck up her vacation.

Guy   But she's unreachable.

Buddy (*deadly*)   What?

Beat.

Guy   Well, she's rafting. In the water. She's afloat. I – I don't imagine they have connection or – or computers there.

Beat.

Buddy   Dawn, excuse me, I just need to train my dickless assistant for a second, please forgive the insolence.

Buddy *heads up to his office and slings open the doors, surprising a terrified* **Cleaner**.

Buddy   Out! Out! Who do you work for?

The **Cleaner** *flees as* **Buddy** *disappears into his office.*

Dawn   What is he, in one of his moods?

Guy   He has other moods?

Dawn *chuckles.* **Guy** *smiles.* **Buddy** *reappears in the doorway of his office. Behind him, an award has been prominently placed on his desk. He smiles at* **Dawn**, *turns to* **Guy**, *and points to a spot on the floor by the door.*

Buddy   Stand there.

Guy *does.*

Buddy   Your feet are lead.

Guy   What?

Buddy   That's all you need to remember. Your feet are lead. Now. See that award?

Guy   Yes.

Buddy   You like it?

Guy   Yeah.

Buddy   What does it feel like?

Guy   I don't know.

Buddy   Touch it.

Guy *steps toward the award.*

Buddy   Your feet are lead!

Guy *steps back.*

Buddy   Touch it.

Guy   But –

Buddy   Touch it. Stretch.

Guy *stretches out his arms toward the award.*

Buddy   Further.

Guy   I can't.

Buddy   Then that, Guy, is 'unreachable'. And that's the way those are gonna stay if you use that fucking word in my office again. You understand?

Guy   Yes, sir.

Buddy   So find Stella. GPS, helicopters, whatever it takes. Now, task two. There's three hundred *Hammertooth* DVDs downstairs waiting for awards mail-out. There's been report of mis-syncing on a couple. I need you to fetch them, watch them, check and see if it's true.

Guy   Watch them?

Buddy   Yeah.

Guy   All of them?

Buddy   Yes, all of them, is that a problem?

Guy   No.

Buddy   Good. 'Cause you'll be doing it for every batch that comes in this year. Now, get.

Guy *scurries toward the exit. On his way out, he catches* **Dawn***'s eye and blinks away in shame.* **Buddy** *notices this.*

Buddy   And take down any messages, Guy. Ms Lockard and I don't want to be disturbed.

Buddy *tosses him his cellphone.*

Guy   Yes, sir.

Buddy   Dawn. Gorgeous. Sit that cute little butt down.

Guy *exits.* **Dawn** *sits on the sofa.* **Buddy** *sits near* **Dawn***.*

Buddy   So, Dawn. What brings you this high up? Life in the independents finally got too cold for you?

Dawn   It's heating up, Buddy.

Buddy   It'd have to, in that dress. Come on, Dawn. You've been away from me too long. Come back to my team, make some real movies.

Dawn   Fat chance, Buddy. I've served my time. Who's the new kid?

Buddy   Looks kind of retarded, doesn't he?

Dawn   I don't know.

Buddy   Fuckin' hick. Some mongrel Rex found. Nailed the test, apparently, highest score ever. Claims to want to be a writer.

Dawn   A writer?

Buddy   Yeah. All I can tell, though, his head's a fucking air vent. I've seen more spunk on Paris Hilton.

Dawn   Charming.

Buddy   Oh, give it up, Dawn. It's a man's game, this town, and you know it.

Dawn   I'm not sure Stella would agree.

Buddy   What the fuck does she have to do with anything? Come on. Come back. The big leagues. You know you want to. (*Beat.*) I might even let you co.

Dawn   Fuck you.

Buddy   Seriously. Let's talk about it. My place. Say, midnight?

Dawn   I'm not one of your dime girls, Buddy.

Buddy   Not one of mine, no.

Dawn   Careful.

Beat.

Buddy   I always had a soft spot for you, you know.

Dawn   That's because I never put out.

Buddy   The only one. (*Beat.*) So why are you here then? If you haven't come to, uh –

Dawn   I said careful, Buddy –

Buddy   Tick the last box. The last exec in Hollywood unbrightened by the Dawn.

Dawn   I've got a project for you.

Buddy   Why me?

Dawn   It's big. A long shoot abroad and it can't be HD. Big sets, big set pieces. I need studio backing.

Buddy   Sounds hot. Who's shooting?

Dawn   The writer. Daniel Faruk.

Buddy   First-timer?

Dawn   Second. Come on. Daniel Faruk? Trademarked the hottest fuckin' thing in the world after last weekend. You didn't see his picture?

Buddy   What do you think?

Dawn   It's amazing. And it's nationwide. Intelligent, entertaining, politically charged –

Buddy   Redeeming, worthwhile?

Dawn   I notice it beat all the blood-drenched male-macho bullshit you boys spewed out.

Buddy   Christmas is a bad time for me. Guilt and goodwill, my fuckin' kryptonite. And excuse me, but this Halloween season my blood-drenched male-macho bullshit broke a hundred and eighty mil. I won't even mention the DVD sales, you'd blush.

Dawn   Please.

Buddy   One eighty. The last important film this studio made peaked at eighteen. Most of which was UK or someplace, Canada, the fuckin' provinces. What's this opus even called?

Dawn   *The Afghani Incident.*

Buddy   No no no no no no no, Dawn. Don't you know me at all? A politico? No one's interested in that.

Dawn   You're a dinosaur, Buddy.

Buddy   Says who?

Dawn   The last of a dying breed and you know it. Times are changing. Anyone can shoot now. Films are coming out on the fucking internet, people are going to get picky.

Buddy   Bullshit.

Dawn   It's the truth. Democracy's comin' in and kids want clever now. So unless you cater to the market, Buddy, the studios will become obsolete. You will become obsolete.

Buddy   It's a fad, Dawn, same as the rest.

Dawn   Then you ought to be riding it. George Clooney is a hero. Clooney. Not James Cameron. Time's overtaking you, Buddy. You need this. It's an important film for the eighteen to twenty-fivers.

Buddy   The eighteen to twenty-fivers are my fucking children, Dawn.

Dawn   Not anymore. They want –

Buddy   I tell them what they want. I know it better than they do, and two years before they're old enough to fuckin' guess. I tell them what they want, Dawn.

Dawn   And what is that?

Buddy   A satisfied appetite. Structures they're used to, straight sensationalism and a night without any fucking questions.

Dawn   Is that so?

Buddy   It is.

Beat.

Dawn   At least read it.

Beat.

Buddy   My place. Midnight. Bring the script. Then I'll read it.

Beat.

Dawn   Fine, if that's how you're playing, I'll take it to Stella.

She stands.

Buddy   Wait. (*Beat.*) *The Afghani Incident.*

Dawn   *The Afghani Incident.*

Pause.

Buddy   No. You have too much faith in people, Dawn. No one wants to think. They want to feel. Visceral, not provocative. This little trend will sink without a trace.

Dawn   You're wrong.

Guy *enters, out of breath and carrying a leaden box of DVDs.*

Buddy   Am I? Let's see. (*To* **Guy**.) You're young, right?

Guy   Yeah, I guess, I'm –

Buddy I don't want your life history, moron, I want yeses and nos. Ms Lockard and I have a little bet.

Guy (*indicating the box*) Can I just –

Buddy In a minute.

Guy It's real heavy.

Buddy So. Picture this. You're stumbling home, a couple of drinks after a hard day drooling down your Teflon suit and you want to take your mind off things. So, you head to the movie store –

Guy Uh –

Buddy What?

Guy I order online.

Dawn You see?

Buddy Let me finish. You get to the store, you head to new releases. And right there, right at eye level 'cause that's where we can afford to place them, you see the latest Keystone flick. Snappy cover, punching in at ninety minutes, regulation. Which genre?

Guy I don't know. Action.

Buddy It's Matt Damon, covered in five stars from every fuckin' journal in our pay range, which is all of them. Michael Bay directing, Michael fuckin' Bay. There are fifty copies in front of you. You look left, you look right, it's all you can see. Until suddenly, out of the corner of your eye, in the bottom row you spy a lone, lonely, dark little cover. The single review reads 'important'. You remember back to the seven days of its theater release, when you were just too busy to make it but you can't quite remember why. You look up again. Fifty bright lights guiding your way to escape. It's a self-checkout, Guy. No one's watching. No one's judging. What do you pick?

Guy Honestly?

Buddy   Honestly.

Guy *looks at* **Dawn** *and then back at* **Buddy**. *Beat.*

Guy   I'd pick the politico.

Buddy   Bullshit.

Dawn (*to* **Guy**)   Thank you. (*To* **Buddy**) See?

Buddy   Why?

Guy   Because I'm not a kid anymore. And movies matter to me.

Beat.

Buddy   Well, thank you, Guy. I won our bet.

Guy   Really?

Buddy   Yeah. You are a fucking retard. Take it to Stella, Dawn, I don't care, I know this business better than he knows how to piss.

Guy *heads to his desk and puts down the box.*

Dawn   You'll regret this, Buddy.

Buddy   I regret nothing. Who called?

Guy (*handing* **Buddy** *back his cellphone*)   Oh, um, OK, uh, Mitzy, Rob, and Cyrus.

Buddy   Cyrus? Cyrus?

Guy   You – you said you didn't want to be disturbed. I didn't think –

Buddy   You didn't think? My meeting's tonight and you didn't think? What good are you? Do you have a brain? Do you want to keep this job? Shut up, listen, learn. Fuck didn't think, fuck your opinion, and fuck you. Fuck you. You are a worthless fuckin' piece of –

Dawn   Well, isn't this turning into an intelligent conversation?

Buddy   Loud and nasty, that's the only way it sticks, Dawn.

Dawn   You did say, 'Take down any messages,' Buddy. And I certainly hope you wouldn't want anyone to intrude on our time together.

Buddy *smiles.*

Buddy   Mmm-hmm. (*To* **Guy**.) Find Cyrus, get him on the phone. If he's not on the line by lunchtime, you'd better not be here either.

Guy *scurries toward his desk and picks up the phone.* **Buddy** *stands.*

Buddy   I'm sorry, Dawn. But you have too much faith. It's a pass.

Dawn (*standing*)   Your loss, Buddy.

Buddy   My loss is squeezin' outta that dress right now.

Dawn   Yeah, so. Kiss it goodbye.

Buddy   Just give me the word.

Dawn   I'll give you two.

Guy   Cyrus on one.

Buddy *heads toward his office.*

Buddy   Good luck with the flick, Dawn. Call me when you got something hot.

Dawn   Last chance, Buddy.

Buddy   We'll see.

Buddy *disappears into his office, frosting the windows.* **Dawn** *composes herself and looks at* **Guy**.

Guy (*into phone*)   Buddy Ackerman's office calling.

Dawn   Buddy's meeting Cyrus tonight?

Guy   Yeah. (*Into phone.*) Yes, I'll hold.

Dawn   Listen, about that little misunderstanding, the parking lot. Let me make it up to you. How about lunch?

Guy   Thank you, but I really, I – I can't.

Dawn   Come on.

Guy   I can't.

Dawn   Look, I'm gonna be real blunt here. As much as I hate it, I need Buddy. If he's even got a shot at President of Production, I need my calls to find their way into his phone sheet. I need my scripts to go home with him on the weekends. In short, I need you on my side. OK? See what I'm saying? I don't want to be put on hold over a parking spot, so can we just try this again? Hey, thank you back there. How about lunch?

Guy *hangs up the phone.*

Guy   I'm not allowed to take lunch – um, Buddy doesn't believe in it.

Dawn   Fine, drinks it is. Here's my card. (*She gives him a card.*) Call me when you're done tonight, all right?

Guy   Tonight?

Dawn   That's all right with you, isn't it?

Guy   Oh, yeah. It just seems that a woman as – as powerful and as attractive and – as pleasant-natured as yourself would be booked up for tonight.

Dawn   Well, guess what, I am now. (*She goes to leave and turns back.*) You know what, piece of advice, you should talk to him about the yelling. 'Cause it really kind of makes you look like a schmuck.

Dawn *leaves.* **Guy** *stares after her. Pause. He looks up at* **Buddy**'s *frosted windows. Pause. He stands, approaches, and knocks, tentative. The windows defrost.*

Buddy   Oh, good, it's you. Listen, tomorrow morning on your way in I want you to stop and pick up a prescription for me. It's some pretty sensitive stuff, so keep it quiet, OK? Try not to screw up. Details are all here.

Buddy *hands* **Guy** *a note, picks up a file on his desk, and begins reading. Beat. He notices* **Guy** *lingering.*

Buddy   Yeah, what?

Guy   Well, I – uh – I wanted to talk to you about the phone calls.

Buddy   No apology necessary, everyone's allowed at least one mistake, you've used up yours, let's not dwell on it.

Guy   Well, that's just it, see, I – I don't feel that I made a mistake.

Buddy *looks up.*

Guy   And, well, I would appreciate it if you didn't yell at me in front of the visiting producers.

Buddy   Excuse me, what?

Guy   Uh, the yelling, I –

Buddy   Oh, you . . . disapprove? I'm sorry. Did I – (*he puts down his reading*) did I hurt your feelings before?

Guy   No, no, no –

Buddy   I was just acting up – bad-cop, you know?

Guy   No, no, listen –

Buddy   I mean, I don't want to be excessive.

Guy   I just don't feel that it's necessary. It certainly doesn't help me, and I –

Buddy   Well, I'm glad you brought this up.

Guy   Really?

Buddy   Because I've found that an office can't run properly if the lines of communication aren't open. You know?

Guy   Right, right, yes.

Buddy   So, in that case, let's make a few things clear.

Guy   OK, great, great, this is helpful, I mean –

Buddy   Let's review. What did I tell you the first day?

Beat.

Guy   Um –

Buddy   Your thoughts are nothing. You are nothing. And yet you have the nerve to walk into my office and tell me that –

Guy   I – I –

Buddy   Please, shut up. At least allow me the courtesy of finishing what I have to say, that's the very least that you can do after I've had to endure your insults.

Guy (*turning to leave*)   This is a bad time.

Buddy (*shooting to his feet*)   Who do you think you are, you snot-faced little punk? Let me make this clear for you, OK, and now try to follow me, because I'm going to be moving in a kind of circular motion, but if you pay attention, there will be a point. You are nothing. If you were in my toilet bowl I wouldn't bother flushing. My bathmat means more to me than you. (*Holds up a file.*) See this? This means more to the office than you. And yet do you hear any complaints when I do this? (*Throws file at* **Guy**.) These pencils more important – (*Throws pencils at* **Guy**.) These pens more important – (*Throws pens at* **Guy**.) These paper clips more important – (*Throws paper clips at* **Guy**.) You miserable little crybaby. You don't like it here, leave. There are thousands of people who would kill for your spot, who would kill for the opportunity to be here. I could spit and hit somebody who could do this job better than you. This is a fast track to the top, boy, I don't see you breaking any speed records. Why can't you show a little backbone, huh, huh? You want to scrape around the girls makin' fuckin' weepies the rest of your life, or do you want to get with the big boys and build movies with balls? Huh? 'I don't think the yelling is necessary.' You got to be a little more thick-skinned, you turd, you got to be a man to do this job.

Guy *makes it out the door just as* **Buddy** *throws another file. The file hits the door. Finally alone,* **Buddy** *chuckles to himself, stretches and yawns.*

Buddy   God, time for breakfast.

Buddy *exits.* **Guy** *re-enters and repeats the following mantra quietly to himself.*

Guy   *The Departed. Crash. Million Dollar Baby. Lord of the Rings* colon *Return of the King. Chicago. A Beautiful Mind. Gladiator. American Beauty. Shakespeare in Love. Titanic. The English Patient. Braveheart. Forrest Gump. Schindler's List. Unforgiven. Silence of the Lambs. Dances with Wolves. Driving Miss Daisy. Rain Man. The Last Emperor. Platoon. Out of Africa. Amadeus. Terms of Endearment. Gandhi. Chariots of Fire. Ordinary People. Kramer vs. Kramer. The Deer Hunter. Annie Hall. Rocky. One Flew Over the Cuckoo's Nest. The Godfather Part II. The Sting. The Godfather. The French Connection. Patton. Midnight Cowboy. Oliver* exclamation mark. *In the Heat of the Night. A Man for All Seasons. The Sound of Music. My Fair Lady. Tom Jones. Lawrence of Arabia. West Side Story. The Apartment. Ben-Hur. Gigi. The Bridge on the River Kwai. Around the World in Eighty Days. Marty. On the Waterfront. From Here to Eternity. The Greatest Show on Earth. An American in Paris. All About Eve. All the King's Men. Hamlet. Gentleman's Agreement. The Best Years of Our Lives. The Lost Weekend. Going My Way. Casablanca. Mrs Miniver. How Green Was My Valley. Rebecca. Gone with the Wind. You Can't Take It with You. The Life of Emile Zola. The Great Ziegfeld. Mutiny on the Bounty. It Happened One Night. Cavalcade. Grand Hotel. Cimarron. All Quiet on the Western Front. The Broadway Melody. Wings.*

Scene Three

A bar, that night. **Guy** *looks around, alone, possibly finishing the mantra from the end of the previous scene.* **Dawn** *approaches.*

Guy   I think this is the coolest bar I've ever seen. It's like *Casablanca,* or −

Dawn   Shhh.

Guy   What?

Dawn   It stops being cool as soon as you say it. What are you having?

Guy   Whatever you have.

Dawn *signals over her shoulder for two drinks. They sit.*

Guy   Talk to him about the yelling? Thanks. That was a good tip.

Dawn   You got to give action to get action. (*Beat.*) So. Guy. What's your story?

Guy   How d'you mean?

Dawn   Is your Uncle Bob in the business?

Guy   No, I –

Dawn   Or are you just another boy out for quick cash, quick cars, and an easy lay?

Guy   Well, let me see. I haven't been paid yet.

Dawn   Right.

Guy   My car's a – what was it? A red-tin –

Dawn   Piece of shit.

Guy   Right.

Dawn   With ass plates.

Guy   With ass plates, right. So I'm not here for the car. And I have never had an easy lay.

Dawn   It shows.

Guy   Jesus. How?

Dawn   You look scared.

Beat.

Guy   You got me here for target practice, is that it?

Dawn   No, I'm just feeling extra charitable.

Guy   Christ.

The drinks arrive.

Dawn   So, come on, talk. Amuse me. What's your story?

Guy   I'm a recent film-school graduate with fairly disappointed middle-class parents.

Dawn   That's hot.

Guy   Parents who hoped their son would be anything but a writer.

Dawn   Oh, you're a writer, really?

Guy   Yeah, one day.

Dawn   A one-day writer.

Guy   That's the dream.

Dawn   Why then, pray tell, are you fetching coffee for Buddy Ackerman?

Guy   Fetching? I'm not fetching.

Dawn   I don't know.

Guy   And he's one of the top studio executives in the business.

Dawn   For now. So you're substituting liberal amounts of ass-kissing for actual talent. Am I right?

Guy   OK, you know what? I've taken just about enough character assassination for one day. (*He stands.*) Thank you for the drink –

Dawn   Would you please sit down? Stop being a girl. (*Beat.*) Come on, sit.

He does.

Guy   Sorry.

Dawn   Never apologize. It's a sign of weakness.

Guy   Sounds like Buddy.

Dawn   It is Buddy. Look, if this time can be spent convincing you into doing anything else with your life, into getting out while you are still whole, then it is time well spent. Let me ask you something. Why do you want this?

Guy   Why do you?

Dawn   That's not the question.

Guy   Come on. I'll show you mine.

Dawn   Why do I want this?

Guy   Yeah.

Dawn   I don't.

Guy   What?

Dawn   I don't want the same as you. The big leagues are full of assholes. Full of men. I just want to make good films.

Guy   Like the Daniel Faruk?

Dawn   Exactly.

Guy   I'd love to read it.

Dawn   Why?

Guy   It sounds great.

Dawn   Don't bullshit me, Guy.

Guy   I'm not.

Dawn   You're the Ackerman assistant.

Guy   So? So were you.

Dawn   No, I was a temp.

Guy   What's the difference?

Dawn   Between me and you? I left the first chance I could.

Guy   How d'you get out?

Dawn   Sacrifice. I made myself available for other opportunities, got what I wanted, and I split.

Guy   What did you want?

Dawn   The ability to dictate my own terms. (*Beat.*) Anyway, Daniel's script's hot. I'm not giving it to anyone I don't trust.

Guy   You can trust me.

Dawn *laughs.*

Dawn   You're serious.

Guy   Of course.

Beat.

Dawn   What are you doing here, Guy?

Guy   You asked me to come.

Dawn   No. Here. Hollywood.

Guy   It's just something that I've always wanted to do.

Dawn   Oh, please.

Guy   No. I'm like you, I want to make decent movies.

Dawn   When?

Guy   Now.

Dawn   Then quit. Write.

Guy   I need the experience. I'll quit in a year, when I know the business.

Dawn   Money and girls, same as the rest.

Guy   No.

Dawn   Then why?

Guy   Do you really want to know?

Dawn   I really want to know.

Guy   Are you going to form some conclusion?

Dawn   No, I really want to know.

Guy   You really want to know?

Dawn   I want to know.

Guy   All right, fine. Memories.

Dawn   Memories.

Guy   Yeah. All my favorite memories have been movies.

Dawn   How do you mean?

Guy   My first toy gun. *Unforgiven*, 1992. All my friends wanted to be Billy the Kid, I was Bill Munny. Used to light fake matches off my fake stubble all through recess, you know? Walk into doors I was squinting so hard. (*Beat.*) My first job, summer '98, sweeping corridors at my local college. *Good Will Hunting* out on rental. Every floor I mopped made me a mathematical genius.

Dawn *smiles.*

Guy   My first car. The summer that *Highway Tracks* opened.

Dawn   I love that picture.

Guy   Me too. Introduced me to the road movie. White-line fever. Still think of it every time I get in a car, you know? A fine Buddy Ackerman movie, come to think of it.

Dawn   An early Buddy Ackerman movie. (*Beat.*) First girl you saw naked.

Guy   Uh, summer of '94. Robin Wright.

Dawn   What was she like?

Guy   Jenny in *Forrest Gump*. Remember? With the guitar?

Dawn   I meant in the flesh.

Guy   I couldn't speak for hours after that movie. Blood, gone from my head.

Dawn   OK. First actual kiss.

Guy   Actual kiss?

Dawn   Actual kiss.

Guy   That would be, uh – '93. I took her to see *Philadelphia*. Made me look sensitive.

Dawn   What was her name?

Guy   I don't remember. But Banderas is amazing in that movie. First time I ever realized that turtleneck is Hollywood for homosexual.

Dawn *laughs.*

Guy   Wow. A smile. Maybe you don't hate me.

Dawn   Wow. Get over yourself.

Guy   My dad and I used to watch the Oscars every year, you know?

Dawn   Me too.

Guy   No shit?

Dawn   Never missed it.

Guy   Me neither.

Dawn   What'd he do?

Guy   You interested?

Dawn   Yeah.

Guy   He was an architect. Small-scale homes, that sort of thing.

Dawn   Good with his hands.

Guy   Yeah. Not like me. But Mom was really the breadwinner, you know? The success.

Dawn   What'd she do?

Guy   She sold them. (*Beat.*) Happiest times I can think of, movies. (*Beat.*) It's all I really remember smiling about after, uh . . .

Dawn   After what?

Beat.

Guy   No. Nothing.

Dawn   What?

Guy   Well, I was going to say after my mom got sick.

Dawn   Oh. I'm sorry.

Guy   But – can I tell you something?

Dawn   Sure.

Guy   She never got sick. I just tell people that.

Dawn   Why?

Guy   I don't know. *Terms of Endearment* won in '84, two years after I was born. Most dramatic thing I can remember.

Beat.

Dawn   You're twenty-four.

Guy   Good math.

Dawn   Thank you.

Guy   How old are you?

Dawn   Nice try. (*Beat.*) I used to tell people I taught my dad to read. (*They smile at each other.*) Piece of advice, Guy. You let Buddy get his claws into you, you'll never be a writer. You understand? You'll never leave. Especially if he gets a sniff that you got any actual talent. He'll tie you to him like roots to the earth. Trust me. You got to make sure you really want what you think you want.

Guy   Are you watching my back, Dawn?

Dawn   Maybe I am.

Beat. **Guy** *leans in and gently kisses* **Dawn**. *She doesn't pull away, but doesn't return.* **Guy** *pulls back. Beat.*

Dawn   If you want to make it in this business, Guy, you don't have room for a personal life.

Guy   OK.

Beat.

Dawn   Much less a relationship.

Guy   Absolutely no relationships, no.

Dawn   Absolutely no relationships. (*Beat.*) I don't like this bar.

Guy   Me either.

Dawn   Let's get out of here.

Dawn *stands and turns to leave.* **Guy** *follows. A soundscape builds recalling the themes of iconic screen romances –* Doctor Zhivago, Love Story, *and* Goodbye, Mr Chips. *This suggests the initial progress of a relationship, and so the passage of time.*

Scene Four

Keystone, late that night. Dim lights. **Buddy**'s *door is cracked open a couple of inches.* **Cyrus** *enters.*

Cyrus   Buddy?

Buddy *appears in his office doorway, surprised.*

Buddy   Cap'n Miles.

Cyrus   Tailwind. I'm early.

Buddy   To real people, Cap'n, this is late.

Cyrus   But not to us.

Buddy   Are you kidding? I'm working all weekend. Here till Monday.

Cyrus   You don't change, do you? (*Beat.*) A drink?

Buddy   Coming up.

Buddy *disappears into his office.* **Cyrus** *sits on the sofa.* **Buddy** *reappears with two glasses of whiskey, closing his office doors behind him.*

Cyrus   Sit, sit. (**Buddy** *does.*) I haven't seen you since Halloween, have I, Buddy?

Buddy   Actually –

Cyrus   I've been meaning to say, congratulations. A real barnstormer.

Buddy   Thank you, sir.

Beat.

Cyrus   You're humoring me.

Buddy   We had lunch the week after, Cap'n. Remember? New York? Chateaubriand was cold, you threw it at the waiter?

Cyrus   I'm getting old, Buddy. Forget things all the time, it seems, all the time. My stature, though, you come to realize it doesn't matter. Forget my own name and no one'd say a goddamn thing. It's a cocoon of smiles.

Buddy   Sounds good to me.

Cyrus   Does it? (*Beat.*) Well, I don't care if I've said it already, congratulations. You paid for my birthday vacation.

Buddy   What was it? The big five-zero?

Cyrus   No.

Buddy   Forty?

Cyrus   Don't tease an old man, Buddy. It's not kind.

Buddy   It's the tan, sir. Too damn brown to be your age.

Beat.

Cyrus   You got a real feel for the people, you know that? The common touch.

Buddy   Hey, I just wanted to hit one for the team. Halloween's a gimme.

Beat.

Cyrus   Well, Buddy. You can guess why I'm here.

Buddy   You said it was urgent.

Cyrus   That's right.

Buddy   And, well, Matthew –

Cyrus   Yes. Ugly business. (*Beat.*) It's taken half his other lung now, but he just keeps on fighting.

Buddy   He's a stayer, all right. (*Beat.*) I've worked for you since I was twenty-four, sir. Been here fifteen-odd years.

Cyrus   Good years.

Buddy   Great years. Great. So, respectfully, Cap'n, I thought you might be about to suggest a change.

Cyrus   You're right.

Buddy   I thought so.

Beat.

Cyrus   Buddy. I think I'm going to make Stella President of Production.

Beat.

Buddy   Sir?

Cyrus   You heard.

Beat.

Buddy   Why?

Cyrus   I don't know. No, that's not true. I do know. You remember my grandson?

Buddy   Joshua.

Cyrus   Just graduated from NYU.

Buddy   Yeah.

Cyrus   Well. He's angry, Buddy. I love the boy, but he won't talk to me. He says I'm ruining the country. Ruining the world with my films. It's rich, considering I paid for the boy's education. But something in me – I don't know. Maybe he's right. Maybe the world is going to hell.

Buddy   Sir –

Cyrus   A hell I'm helping to build.

Buddy   He's a child, sir.

Cyrus   They'll inherit the earth, Buddy. Not you. Certainly not me.

Buddy   But Cap'n, the figures – Halloween –

Cyrus   That's indisputable, but –

Buddy   That was all me, Cyrus. Me. I know what people want, you said –

Cyrus   Well, maybe we shouldn't be giving them what they want. Maybe we should be teaching them a thing or two. (*Beat.*) Joshua told me about this latest one you've been doing – some horror picture with an eyeball and a pair of scissors. Household appliances, Buddy. Who knows what would happen if a child saw that?

Buddy   Come on, sir, no one takes these pictures seriously. Did you think you had no heart because you saw the Tin Man? It's escapism, it's fantasy.

Cyrus   Well, I want them to take me seriously, Buddy. It's not a fantasy I want to indulge any longer. (*Beat.*) Stella's making decent movies. Worthwhile movies. This new character, Joshua's hero, Daniel Faruk, is it? Independent type.

Buddy   Opened last weekend.

Cyrus   You know his work?

Buddy   Entertaining, politically charged.

Cyrus   Well, Stella's courting him. That's where we should be looking. That's the future.

Buddy   That and the poorhouse.

Cyrus   Maybe you're right. But it's my legacy, Buddy. And I know it sounds grand, but I want to bequeath the world something noble.

Buddy   At least give me a chance.

Cyrus   You're out of your depth here. You're a specialist.

Buddy   So is Stella. Sure, she can sell decency to France, to the black 'n' whites and art houses. But I know America, sir, I know the people. You said it yourself, the common touch.

Cyrus   True.

Buddy   So give me a chance. (*Beat.*) Fifteen years.

Beat.

Cyrus   What do you have in mind?

Buddy   I'll make you something decent. My next picture. Something noble.

Cyrus   So will Stella.

Buddy   Sure, but mine will crack fifty mil. Guaranteed. (*Beat.*) Hold off on the decision. My next picture.

Beat.

Cyrus   OK. For you.

Buddy   Thank you. Thank you, Cyrus.

Cyrus   I can stall the board for six months, tell Stella tomorrow. Gives both of you a chance to get something big ready for Oscar season. But that's it, Buddy. Six months. If she outperforms you –

Buddy   Fair's fair.

Cyrus   Quality, not just gross.

Buddy   Just give me a shot. Come on. What are you going to do, bequeath something noble to the French?

Cyrus   No. You're right. America's all that really counts.

Buddy   Amen to that.

Cyrus   Amen indeed.

He stands and hands **Buddy** *his whiskey glass.*

Cyrus   I don't think I ever said how sorry I was about your wife.

Buddy   Thank you.

Cyrus   Awful, the whole business. That that can happen to a man.

Buddy   It was meant to happen, Cap'n.

Cyrus   You really believe that?

Buddy   I wouldn't be here if things hadn't worked out the way they did. Wouldn't have had the time.

Cyrus   Yes. You look a wreck.

Buddy   Thank you.

Cyrus   Your hair's thinning.

Buddy   Hey. I don't have something to piss me off, I'm not happy.

Beat.

Cyrus   Thank you for the drink, Buddy. And good luck.

Cyrus *leaves.* **Buddy** *walks up to his office and opens the door, revealing* **Mitzy**.

Mitzy   Are you coming back to play?

Buddy   Get out.

Mitzy   What?

Buddy   Out. Now.

Beat. Unnerved, **Mitzy** *collects her things and hurries out of the office.* **Buddy** *stands alone.*

Scene Five

Keystone. Early Monday morning. The office is empty and silent. The windows of **Buddy**'s *office are frosted over, and* **Buddy** *is nowhere to be seen. The phone rings. Beat.*

Suddenly, **Guy** *rushes in, haggard, flustered, and carrying a Starbucks coffee, a pharmacy bag, a* Hollywood Reporter, *and a script. The phone stops ringing just as he reaches it. He rests his head on the desk in frustration, and pounds it once, violently. The force is surprising. He then starts up in panic and checks the time. He looks around. No one. He looks up at* **Buddy**'s *office. No one. Slowly, not believing his luck,* **Guy** *walks to his desk and sits down in his chair. He puts his feet on his desk and reclines, hands behind his head. He closes his eyes. Beat.*

Buddy *silently emerges from the kitchenette, stirring a cup of coffee. He looks tired but charged. He stares at* **Guy**, *who remains peacefully unaware. Slowly,* **Buddy** *advances.*

Buddy   I haven't made my own coffee –

Guy *snaps out of his slumber and scrambles to assume composure, pulling a file from a stack on his desk and beginning to read diligently.*

Buddy   – since 1993. It was midnight. I was just about to leave the office when my boss had a breakdown. He told me to make sure that every single document in the archive was stapled at exactly the same angle. By the morning. I worked through the night, a cup an hour. I needed it just to survive, Jesus, I'd been working forty hours straight when he gave me the damn job. The last time I made my own coffee. Nineteen ninety-three. Fourteen years ago. And still –

Buddy *slowly pours his coffee onto* **Guy***'s file. The coffee splashes on* **Guy***'s hands.*

Guy   Christ –

Buddy   Still, this cup of piss tastes twice as good as the poison that you serve me every single day. (*He finishes pouring the coffee.*) You're late.

Guy   I'm sorry.

Buddy   Are you? What have you got there?

Guy   Where?

Buddy   There, in the cup.

Guy   Oh, that's, uh, that's a Starbucks. (*Beat.*) Would you like it?

Buddy   Could I? (*He picks up the cup.*) Now, Guy, let me ask you a question. If you were really sorry, would you have taken the time to get this? Hmm? Christ, if you're going to lie, at least make it credible. You're like a narcotized ape this morning.

Guy   Yeah, I, uh, I had a late night.

Buddy   Past twelve? Grow some balls. Now, next job, top priority. Find out what Stella's reading and get me a copy.

Guy   Stella?

Buddy   Yes, Stella.

Guy How?

Buddy   What do I care? Go undercover, fuck her assistant.

Guy   Derek?

Buddy   Buy a dress. (*He sips the Starbucks and immediately spits it back out over* **Guy**.) Oh, God, what the hell is this?

Guy   It's a latte.

Buddy   A what?

Guy   A latte.

Buddy   Christ alive, Jimmy, go easy or you'll get the shakes. You can keep this. (*He hands the cup back to* **Guy** *and heads back toward his office.*) Make me a real cup, black, and thick as tar. Then pack me up. I got services in half an hour.

Guy   Services? Who died?

Buddy   No one. Yet. It's Passover, you idiot.

Guy   Oh. I didn't realize Ackerman was a Jewish name.

Buddy   It's Jewish enough. Especially when Cyrus is involved. Besides, I feel a sudden need to atone for my sins.

Buddy *enters his office.* **Guy** *jogs toward the kitchenette, but is interrupted by the ringing of his cellphone. He answers, sotto voce, taking a towel from the kitchenette and mopping up the coffee on his desk as he talks.*

Guy (*into phone*)   Hello? (*Beat.*) Hey. (*Beat.*) I know, I feel like I'm on fire. Can I see you tonight? (*Beat.*) I know I did, but I miss you already. Three days and I'm hooked. (*Beat.*) The script? It's great, I – (*Beat.*) Of course I won't show it to anyone. Come on, what do you think I am?

Buddy *appears in the doorway of his office carrying a script.*

Guy (*into phone*)   OK, that's –

Buddy *hurls the script at* **Guy**. **Guy** *looks up, startled and confused.*

Buddy   You're happy. I hate that. Get off the phone and get in here.

He disappears back into his office.

Guy (*into phone*)   I have to go. Dinner at your place? (*Beat.*) Perfect.

He hangs up, picks the pharmacy bag and Hollywood Reporter *up off his desk, and scurries into* **Buddy**'s *office.*

Buddy   Who was that?

Guy   Oh – uh – no one.

Buddy   Are you taking personal calls on my time?

Guy   No, I –

Buddy   I don't pay you to sit and chat, Guy. You talk for me.

Guy   No, it was for you, it was –

Buddy   I heard 'dinner'. I heard 'your place'. Am I having dinner with someone? At their place? Sounds romantic, Guy, but I'd appreciate it if you'd let me know these things, because –

Guy   It was no one.

Buddy   Good. Keep it that way. (*Indicating the pharmacy bag.*) What's that?

Guy   Your Rogain, and your, uh –

Buddy   Great. Put it in the cabinet.

Guy *exits to the executive bathroom.*

Guy (*offstage*)   I don't get it. You're not losing your hair.

Buddy   Exactly. Anticipate.

Guy *reappears carrying a gun.*

Guy   You have a gun?

Buddy   Like I said. Anticipate. Put it back. (**Guy** *does so.*) What's happening?

Guy *reappears and starts loading files into* **Buddy**'s *briefcase.*

Guy   Um, well, there's the *Reporter* article for you to read, and, uh, Rob –

Buddy   What *Reporter* article?

Guy *leafs through the* Hollywood Reporter.

Guy   Well, it's an article on violence in cinema. It says you've promoted yourself from the, uh, 'King of Wham-Bam Action' to the 'Lord of Gore'. Yeah, right here.

He hands **Buddy** *the magazine with the pages open.*

Buddy   Why does nobody tell me these things?

Guy   It only came out an hour ago.

Buddy   Who gave them this picture? Oh, Jesus Christ. Have you read this?

Guy   Yeah.

Buddy   Where do they get these lies? I'm a blight on society? (*He reads.*) Oh, come on, some hick kid in Texas tears his brother's eye out with a meat skewer and I'm responsible? Blame Spielberg for the fuckin' Holocaust. Wait, wait – this is marked internal. Who sent you this?

Guy   Derek.

Buddy   Stella. I knew it. Fine, that bitch wants a war, she'll get one. Battle plan. When's she next open?

Guy   May second.

Buddy   Hold *Bloodball* back a week, up the post on *Grind Three*. Reschedule both for May second, get 'em in every fuckin' theater she's ever seen.

Guy   Both of them?

Buddy   We'll sell it as a head-to-head, get world-to-world coverage. End of the month, Guy, mark my words, no one'll've even sniffed the heartsleeve crap Stella's tryin' to cry out. We're gonna blow that cat out of the fuckin' jungle. (*He looks at the magazine.*) And as for this – we need to kill it, right now. Find every copy in town and destroy it.

Guy   Every copy?

Buddy   Yeah. Every copy. Find it. Bury it.

He tosses the magazine back to **Guy**.

Guy   But it's – it's the *Hollywood Reporter*.

Buddy   So?

Guy   So it's got a circ of twenty-six thousand. And it's online, it's global. It – it would probably be hard to get every copy.

Buddy   Am I your brain, Guy?

Guy   No.

Buddy   So think for yourself. Call the airport, stop the press truck, invent a virus and hit every newsstand in town.

Guy   But –

Buddy   What?

Guy   That'd take all night.

Buddy   So?

Guy   I have plans.

Buddy   Cancel them.

Guy   I can't.

Buddy   Fuck what you can't, this is important.

Guy   I'm sorry, Buddy, I promised Dawn, I –

Buddy *snaps round and stares at* **Guy**.

Guy   Um, I promised –

Buddy   Dawn Lockard?

Guy   Yeah.

Buddy   What are you doing with her?

Guy   We, uh . . . We're –

Buddy   Wait. You look tired. No. Don't tell me . . . No. You two? She's fucking you? Jesus, why?

Guy   I don't know.

Buddy   Why you?

Guy   I think she likes me.

Buddy   She likes you? Jesus. Shut up, listen, learn. This is important. How long have you known her?

Guy   A few days.

Buddy   A few fuckin' hours, most of which you had your head in her ass. This is not the movies, Guy. This is not love at first sight. This is screw or be screwed. Something Dawn knows all too well. She wants something.

Guy   I like her.

Buddy   I like steak, but I don't fuck it. Especially not when every other exec in town has had a bite.

Guy   What do you mean?

Buddy   Ask Dawn what I mean.

Guy   Ask her what?

Buddy   Oh, Christ, it doesn't matter. You want to believe the latest broad to lay down and beg is Snow fuckin' White, be my guest, whatever makes you happy. Just remember this, Guy. Never show anyone the cards in your hand, OK?

Guy   OK.

Buddy   Especially if they say they're not playing.

Buddy *sits, winds up a windup toy, and sets it in motion across his desk.*

Guy   Look, it sounds crazy, I know, we've only just met but −

Buddy   Shhh.

Buddy *points at the windup toy. They wait for it to finish its journey. It does.* **Buddy** *looks at* **Guy**.

Guy   What's – what's up?

Buddy   How do you feel about the past eight weeks, Guy?

Guy   Nine weeks.

Buddy   That long?

Guy   Yes, sir.

Buddy   How have they been?

Guy   For me?

Buddy   Yes, for you.

Beat.

Guy   Well, I think I've been finding my feet a little –

Buddy   I would agree.

Guy   But I think – I hope – I mean, I hope that I'm settling into it.

Buddy   Are you enjoying your time here?

Guy   Yes. Yes, very much.

Buddy   Good. That's good. Because I've wanted to review.

Guy   OK.

Pause.

Buddy   I'm impressed, Guy.

Guy   Excuse me?

Buddy   I'm impressed.

Guy   Really?

Buddy   Sure. I mean, we've had our differences, right?

Guy   Right, yes, a few, but –

Buddy   But nothing that's not attributable to the first stages of a working relationship.

Guy   First stages.

Buddy   Yeah, first stages. Of many, perhaps. Who knows?

Guy   I don't know.

Buddy   No, you don't. Because, as you are aware, this is a high-pressure environment.

Guy   Yes.

Buddy   And you've got to be tough in order to survive.

Guy   Yes.

Buddy   Good. I get a little cranky myself sometimes. The coffee, for example.

Guy   Oh, God, sorry, let me get you –

Buddy   No, no, don't worry about it. But, you see, Guy, after my talk with Cyrus on Friday –

Guy   Oh, Jesus, how did it go?

Buddy   Well. It went very well. Thank you for asking.

Guy   You got the job?

Buddy   What do you think?

Guy   Congratul—

Buddy   But that's got to be our little secret. OK?

Guy   What? Why?

Buddy   McCoy's still breathing – some fuckin' iron lung or something, I don't know, but he's hanging on. The Pooh-Bah's going to stall the announcement for a while. Respect for the wish-you-were-dead, all that crap. But don't you worry. Soon. We'll announce soon.

Guy   Great.

Buddy   And, you see, Guy, I need to distinguish the most dynamic, the most exciting possible players to be on my team. My inner circle. Does that make sense to you?

Guy   Yes – yes it does.

Buddy   So. (*Beat.*) I think it's time you flexed your muscles a little, Guy. I want to give you a shot.

Guy   OK.

Buddy   Does that sound good to you?

Guy   Yeah, that sounds fantastic.

Buddy   But I want it to be something suited to you, to your skills and needs.

Guy   Great. That's great.

Beat.

Buddy   And you're getting along with Dawn.

Beat.

Guy   Yeah.

Buddy   That's good.

Guy   It's great.

Beat.

Buddy   What about her project?

Guy   What project?

Buddy   The Daniel – what's it called?

Guy   Daniel Faruk.

Buddy   That's it, the Daniel Faruk.

Guy   What about it?

Buddy   You think it's got legs?

Guy   Sure, I mean –

Buddy   'Cause I heard her pitch and I thought, 'I can't do this.'

Guy   Yeah.

Buddy   'This is not me. It's not saleable.'

Guy   OK.

Buddy   But you – you seem to be interested.

Guy   I think it's interesting, sure. I just finished reading it on the way in. I mean, it's got credibility problems, but it's serious. It's angry. And funny. Ideology without didacticism, you know? Fury in fun, like Kaufman does Marx.

Beat.

Buddy   Fantastic. (*Beat.*) Tell you what, Guy. I'm going to go out on a limb. Why don't we see what you can do with it? Set it up.

Guy   Set it up?

Buddy   Yeah. Put it together. Budget it, schedule it, locations – set it up, you know? Have some fun. Let's see if you can sell me.

Guy   But –

Buddy   What?

Pause.

Guy   But I can't. It's Dawn's project.

Buddy   So?

Guy   So you passed, she's pissed.

Buddy   Get her unpissed. It's a challenge.

Guy   That's won't be easy.

Buddy   Easy? You're worried about easy? Maybe I was wrong about you.

Guy   No, no, no – I just mean, she's pretty set. She's taking it to Stella in a couple of days, soon as she's back from the water.

Buddy   Has she already taken it?

Guy   No, but the meeting's fixed.

Buddy   Then she's not set.

Guy   I guess.

Buddy   Besides, if you tell me you like her –

Guy   I do like her.

Buddy   Then you really don't have a choice, Guy.

Guy   Why not?

Buddy   Listen, OK? I'm older than you, and I've been married, kid, I know some things. Women? They respond to one thing, and one thing only. Success. Now this isn't just me talking, this is scien— Sit down.

Guy *does.*

Buddy   This is scientific fact. It is primitive instinct for a woman like Dawn to choose a mate who can best provide for her needs. For her wants. Now. It's no offense to you, but you are only an assistant. Sure, I mean, you're my assistant, but, you know, nonetheless. An assistant. Dawn, on the other hand, is a producer. Her cellphone bills are more than your rent. And somebody else pays them. So if you let Dawn take this to Stella, just how long do you think you're going to last?

Guy   Dawn and I, we –

Buddy   All right. No, no, no, I want to help out. Think about it. Why is she with you?

Guy   Because she likes me.

Buddy   Really? Who approached who?

Guy   Well, she –

Buddy   She approached you. Exactly. And what did she say? The first thing?

Guy   She said – she needed me to make sure her calls got through.

Buddy   You see? Now, do you really believe that a rising independent producer of Dawn's stature would have picked you out, out of the blue, just seen the little rookie sitting in the corner and set her sights, would she have done that unless she had something to gain? Do you really believe that?

Guy   I –

Buddy   Of course you don't, Guy, you're not an idiot.

Guy   No.

Buddy   So until Stella says yes, Dawn needs you on her side. Because she still needs me.

Guy   She hates you.

Buddy   Oh, she tells you that, sure, so that you relay it to me and I come back with a higher offer. It's negotiation, Guy, it's like flirting. You'll learn. You're being used as a conduit, as an –

Guy   Instrument?

Buddy   Exactly, a tool. But, see, if you get Dawn to bring this project to me, you're not going to be just an instrument any longer. You set it up, and you'll have a stake in the movie. You'll be on equal terms. Her equal.

Guy   You can do that?

Buddy   She brings it to us, she signs fifty-fifty, no question. But of course, if you let her take it to Stella – well. You're no longer any use, are you? You're stuck here, with me. On the outside.

Beat.

Guy   So all I do –

Buddy   All you do is convince Dawn to bring the project back to me. Not to Stella, to me. See, I could do it, but then there'd be no payoff for you.

Guy   I just don't know how I would –

Buddy   Satisfy her appetite. Work out what she wants and offer it, only up her expectations. Never fails.

Guy   Right.

Buddy   This is what you want, Guy. Isn't it? Making movies, this is what you're here for?

Guy   Yeah, I guess.

Buddy   Good. Because you do this thing, you convince Dawn to go this way, and then you are going to become indispensable, my friend. A solid gold, indispensable, lovable success.

Beat.

Guy   All right. I'll do it.

Buddy   Good. That's good. (*Beat.*) Now, before you do, would you mind fetching me that coffee? I'm bushed. Long weekend, you know?

Guy   I do.

He stands and moves to the door.

Buddy   And make it to go. Services start in fifteen minutes.

Guy   Of course.

Beat. He turns.

Thank you, Buddy.

Buddy   Not at all. Oh, and can you fetch me the script?

Guy   Which script?

Buddy   Your script. You said you were reading it on the way in.

Beat.

Guy   No, sure, I'll just – it's just on my desk.

He exits to the antechamber and picks the script up off his desk. He looks at it, then looks back at **Buddy**'s *office. He heads into the kitchenette, carrying the script.*

Buddy *smiles, stands, picks up his packed briefcase, and exits to the antechamber.* **Guy** *reemerges with a coffee in a to-go cup and the script.* **Buddy** *smiles and takes them both.*

Buddy   And don't forget those articles.

Guy   I won't.

Buddy   Great. That's great. Keep it up, Guy.

Buddy *exits.* **Guy** *is jubilant.*

Scene Six

Keystone, late that night. **Guy** *stands, talking on his cellphone, surrounded by bin bags full of the* Hollywood Reporter.

As he talks he watches one of **Buddy**'s *movies on the flat-screen. The movie flashes red, and we hear the occasional scream or the sound of a drill.*

Guy (*into phone*)   Dawn, I'm sorry, I know it's late, but I – (*Beat.*) Of course I want to be there but I'm nearly done. I'll be there in a half-hour, I promise.

A scream comes from the screen. **Guy** *is disgusted. Beat.*

I'm sorry, what? (*Beat.*) I will. Look, I have to go. (*Beat.*) OK. See you in half an hour.

Buddy *enters in a clinch with* **Mitzy**, *heading toward his office.*

Buddy   . . . just in my office. (*He notices* **Guy** *and halts. Beat.*) What are you doing here? Why aren't you with Dawn?

Guy   The articles.

Buddy   Still?

Guy   I'm just throwing out the last copies now.

Buddy   No, no no no, you can't just throw them out, you have to destroy them.

Guy *looks around him at the stacks of bin bags.*

Guy   But – the mailroom's closed. There's no shredder.

Buddy   So? Rip them up.

Guy   Rip them up?

Buddy   Every copy.

Beat.

Guy   It's just that – it's getting kind of late.

Buddy   Late? What are you, Amish?

Guy   No, but I told Dawn I'd be over in half an hour.

Buddy   So? Finish here, then wake her up.

Guy   But –

Buddy   Oh, I know, things are rough now, but they'll get better, I promise, Guy. Look at me. See?

He heads through his office into his executive bathroom.

(*Offstage.*) If you prove you can manage these tasks, if you work hard now, then you're rewarded. You get to have some fun.

He reemerges carrying the pharmacy bag.

Because don't ever forget, Guy, this job is very big on payback.

Guy   Right. (*Tearing a magazine.*) Payback.

Buddy (*to* **Mitzy**)   Tour's over. My place, Mandy.

Mitzy   Mitzy.

Buddy   A pedant. Who knew? (*To* **Guy**.) Sleep tight.

Guy   You too.

Buddy *and* **Mitzy** *exit. Beat. There is a scream on the screen.* **Guy** *watches, this time unfazed. He picks up his cell and dials.*

Guy (*into phone*)   Dawn? It's me. There's been a change of plan.

Scene Seven

Dawn*'s apartment, later that night. Cicadas chirp outside.* **Dawn***, wrapped in her dressing gown, is asleep in a chair. An open bottle of champagne, two used glasses and some scripts lie next to her on the floor. The doorbell rings.* **Dawn** *wakes up and answers the door.* **Guy** *stands outside with two full bin bags resting by his feet. He produces chocolates from behind his back. He has blood on his hands, but, for now,* **Dawn** *does not notice.*

Guy   Ta-da.

Dawn   I'm still pissed at you.

Guy   I know. I'm sorry. I just needed to see you.

Dawn   I thought you were working.

Guy   I don't care about work. I left early.

Dawn   You call this early?

Guy   For Buddy, yes.

Dawn   Don't mention that name. It's contagious.

Guy   Tell me about it. (*Indicating the bin bags.*) Can I store these here?

Dawn   What are they?

Guy   A labor of love. (*Beat.*) He'd kill me if he found out.

Dawn   Then sure.

She steps aside. **Guy** *drags in the bin bags.*

Guy   I just – I wanted to apologize.

Dawn   Never apologize –

Guy   Sign of weakness, I know. But I don't care. I'm weak. And I'm tired. And I wanted to see you.

Dawn   I'm not playing second string, Guy. I don't have the time to waste on that kind of relationship, OK? If you're with me, you're with me.

Guy   OK. I am. OK? (*Beat.*) Been watching some of the new slate all night, checking the fucking sound sync. My head feels like a hacksaw.

Guy *massages his temples.* **Dawn** *notices the cuts on his hands.*

Dawn   Christ, what's happened to your hands? Did you kill someone?

Guy   I wish. Buddy made me shred some paper. Without a shredder.

Dawn   You let him think he can run your life, he'll get used to it. You'll get used to it, Guy.

Guy   It's the first few weeks. I just – I have to do whatever it takes to make a good impression.

Dawn   I know that feeling.

Guy   Do you.

Dawn   Yeah. It's dangerous.

Guy   Well, I think it's working.

Dawn   In this town, you don't ever think, Guy. You suspect. Especially when it comes to Buddy Ackerman. (*Beat.*) Come on. Let's go to bed. First few weeks with me, too, you know.

She kisses him. Long, seductive. He gently breaks the kiss and holds her. Over her shoulder, he notices the champagne bottle and glasses.

Guy   Have you been celebrating?

Dawn   No. Well, yeah. After you couldn't come, Daniel called, said he wanted to talk through the script.

Guy Oh.

Dawn So he came over and we –

Guy What?

Dawn Talked it through. (*Beat.*) What?

Guy No, nothing.

Dawn You're not jealous, are you?

Guy God, no.

Dawn You've got to be grown up about me, Guy.

Guy I'm being stupid. I'm sorry.

Dawn These people don't look at you unless you give them personal attention.

Guy So I'm told.

Beat.

Dawn Come on.

Guy I'll catch you up.

Dawn Aren't you tired?

Guy Yeah, but I'm not going to sleep, I'm too frazzled. Sorry. I'll finish my notes, be in in a bit.

Dawn What notes?

Guy On *Afghani*.

Dawn It needs notes?

Guy A couple.

Dawn Daniel thinks it's perfect.

Guy It's great. But –

Dawn What?

Beat.

Guy   I just want to help, Dawn.

Beat.

Dawn   God. A man who's interested in my career.

Guy   I don't say what I think, what's the point in talking?

Dawn *smiles. Beat.*

Dawn   You know, I think you might be the only honest man in Hollywood.

Guy   Is that why you like me?

Dawn   Jesus. Screw a twelve-year-old, get playground questions.

Guy   Seriously, Dawn. I don't understand it. I'm an assistant.

Dawn   'Cause I only fuck power.

Guy   No, God, that's not – I'd never think that. It's just – I'm so green.

Dawn   Listen. Guys in Hollywood? Most of them just want to lick you and put you back in the fridge, OK? And we go along with it. It's like the Middle East out here, women are just slaves with smiles.

Guy   Is that why you're making *Afghani*?

Dawn   No, that's why I'm fucking you. Don't be glib.

Guy   Sorry.

Dawn   Everyone expects you to succeed, Guy, you just have to fit the bill, talk the talk, and people'll give you a chance. Women are expected either to fuck or to fail.

Guy   But you're a success.

Dawn   What I'm saying is, with you, I feel different. I'm –

Guy   In charge?

Dawn   I thought you liked playing houseboy.

Guy What?

Dawn   Look at your hands. (*Beat.*) I'm with you, Guy,
because it feels like the right thing.

Guy   This isn't what I want, Dawn. I don't want to do this.

Dawn   What?

Guy   Hollywood.

Dawn   Bullshit.

Guy   The games, houseboy – none of it's real. The whole
fucking rise, I'm spinning, you know? It makes me nauseous.

Dawn   I do know.

Beat.

Guy   Move away with me.

Dawn   What?

Guy   If we could, would you move away with me?

Dawn   Are you insane?

Guy   Back to New York. Or Montana.

Dawn   Montana?

Guy   Yeah, someplace real, someplace outdoors, y'know, with
air. This town's like fog, it's like an island in fog. I feel like –
like if I spend too much time here, I'll start believing that this
is all there is in the world. I can feel myself being fucked, but
I'm not doing anything about it.

Dawn   Welcome to womanhood.

Guy   I'm serious.

Dawn   So am I. I'm not leaving town, Guy.

Guy   Why not?

Dawn   I hardly know you.

Guy   So?

Dawn   So I don't want to quit my job. I suffered to get it.

Guy   You wouldn't have to quit your job. Look, if we had a hit –

Dawn   We?

Guy   Sure.

Dawn   You're an assistant, Guy.

Guy   I know, Christ. But why shouldn't we work together?

Dawn   Why should we?

Guy   We'd be on equal terms.

Dawn   Are you jealous?

Guy   I'm just saying. If we worked together, we'd have no one to please but each other. And then none of this would matter. No houseboy, no personal attention. We'd be on our own terms.

Beat.

Guy   All we'd need is one big movie. Then we could go to Montana, make films from there. Away from this. Away from the assholes.

Dawn   Away from Buddy Ackerman.

Guy   Exactly. Exactly. Away from Stella Smiley.

Dawn   She's one of the good ones, Guy.

Guy   She's the same as the rest.

Dawn   No, she's a woman.

Guy   That makes her different?

Dawn   Yes. It makes her tougher.

Guy   Look, away from all of them. I just – I want to keep you safe from these people, you know?

Dawn   Protect me.

Guy   Yeah.

Dawn   Like a big Montana cowboy.

Guy   Why not?

Dawn   You're sweet, Guy. (*Beat. She picks up a script.*) Look, can you fetch me a glass of wine?

Guy   You're going to work?

Dawn   Sure. If you are.

Guy   On what?

Dawn *shows him the script.*

Guy   I read that, it's a piece of shit.

Dawn   Passed on mid-six last week.

Guy   Jeez.

Dawn   Valuable piece of shit.

Beat.

Guy   It's still a piece of shit, though.

Dawn   The wine, Guy?

Beat. He fetches the wine. She smiles.

Protect and serve. You're so useful.

Beat.

Guy   So what do you think?

Dawn   About what?

Guy   The plan.

Dawn   I like it.

Guy   Then let's do it.

Dawn   Do what?

Guy   With *Afghani*. Let's make it a hit.

Dawn   *Afghani?*

Guy   Yeah.

Dawn   It's already going to be a hit.

Guy   You think?

Dawn   Yeah. Don't you?

Guy   In Europe, sure.

Dawn   But not domestic.

Guy   Come on, Dawn. Stella's not going to sell it over here. She doesn't know how. It's polemic, it's anti-patriotic, it's –

Dawn   Honest?

Guy   Exactly. It's honest. That won't sell America.

Dawn   Well, what do you suggest?

Guy   We take it back to Buddy.

Dawn   What? You just said you wanted away from Buddy.

Guy   Hear me out. Who knows the domestics better than anyone? Huh? Buddy. And who's got a record of turning iron into gold ninety-nine times out of ten? Buddy. It's proved, it's history.

Dawn   I know. Why do you think I went to him in the first place?

Guy   So ask him again.

Dawn   No way.

Guy   Why not?

Dawn   I've moved on. And he passed.

Guy   I could ask him.

Dawn   What?

Guy   He'll listen to me.

Dawn   Bullshit.

Guy   No, no, listen. He said he was impressed with me.

Dawn   Really?

Guy   Yeah. He said he wanted to give me more responsibility. Let me put it together, give him another shot.

Dawn   Are you serious?

Guy   As Schindler. I've thought it through. It's perfect. If I put it together, Buddy can't fuck with it – I won't let him, I'm on the inside. We can dictate our own terms, but we still get made on the scale we wanted. If you go with Stella, you're not in her office, you're not in her head. She'll shut you out, and you stay where you are. We stay where we are.

Dawn   I don't know, Guy.

Guy   Listen to me. And this is top secret, OK? You can't even tell Daniel.

Dawn   What is it?

Guy   You promise?

Dawn   Yeah.

Guy   Buddy's President of Production.

Dawn   What?

Guy   He's got it all wrapped up. Cyrus told him on Friday, they're just waiting for McCoy to croak before they pop the news. By the time *Afghani* gets going, Buddy will be in charge and Stella will be ancient history. You want to make this fly, we have to go with Buddy. (*Beat.*) You got to give action to get action, Dawn. You said it.

Dawn   You don't know the half.

Guy   We make this with Buddy, we won't ever have to see him again, I promise. We just use him to make it huge. An instrument. Then, it's me and you. (*Beat.*) Come on. I'm committed to this.

Dawn   You're young, Guy.

Guy   So?

Dawn   So you're committed to whatever's in front of you.

Guy   What have you got to lose?

Dawn   My integrity, my rep, my relationship with Stella –

Guy   This time next year, you won't even remember her name. Come on. Cancel your meeting with Stella and give me a chance. I'll put it together, assemble a crew. Set it up the way we want it, me and you. Then I'll take it to Buddy. If he says no, he says no.

Dawn   Why are you asking this?

Guy   For us. Top string. (*Beat.*) Don't you trust me?

Pause.

Dawn   OK. Do it.

Guy   Thank you.

Dawn   But just for this one film. We never see Buddy again.

Guy   Of course.

Dawn   And only so long as no changes are made to the script.

Guy   I promise.

Dawn   Absolutely no changes.

Guy   Absolutely no changes, I swear.

Dawn   And I'm solo credit, Guy. Everything comes through me. Buddy's exec, nothing else. No co-producers.

Guy   Of course.

Dawn   And before anything, you've got to convince Daniel. He's sold on Stella, and I'm not going to risk losing him because of Buddy.

Guy   Leave it to me. Thank you, Dawn.

They kiss. Beat.

Dawn   You really think you want to move away with me?

Guy   I'll go wherever you want.

Dawn   Well. (*She puts the script to one side.*) I've got a good idea where you can start.

Dawn *exits to the bedroom, beckoning.* **Guy** *smiles, stands, and follows.*

Scene Eight

Keystone. **Guy** *sits at his desk speaking on the phone.*

Guy (*into phone*)   Mischa, come on. How could Buddy be devoted to anyone but you? (*Beat.*) Well, I'll tell you what you do. You fix yourself a smile and get your cute little butt his place by midnight. (*Beat.*) OK. The key will be under the BAFTA on the doorstep.

Buddy *enters carrying the script of* The Afghani Incident.

Guy (*into phone*)   OK, then. Bye, beautiful.

He hangs up.

Buddy   Did you cancel the meeting with Stella?

Guy   Yeah. Stella was pissed, but –

Buddy   Excellent work, Guy. Divide and conquer.

Guy   Well, I –

Buddy   But I hate the title, I hate the ending, they've got to go.

Guy   No, no, she said no changes.

Buddy   Excuse me?

Guy   Those are the terms. She – uh – Dawn said we could do it only so long as we make absolutely no changes, and we convince Daniel that we're OK.

Beat.

Buddy   All right. We can work with that. Anything else?

Guy   Nikki called, invited you to her birthday in the hills this weekend.

Buddy   How old is she now?

Guy   Seventeen.

Buddy   She is seventeen or she's turning seventeen?

Guy   She is seventeen, turning eighteen.

Buddy   Accept the invitation.

Guy   Now, you had a half-hour free at lunch (*he looks at his watch*) now, so I called Daniel's people and booked him in.

Buddy   Great.

Guy   Just so you know, he thinks you're the people's devil. He was a hundred percent on Stella. Think you can swing him?

Buddy   Christ, Guy, I convince babies they need breast reductions, one rookie fuckin' director's going to be breakfast. When's he here?

Guy   He's waiting, West Lobby.

Buddy   Great. Prep me. Last movie.

Guy   *Remuneration*.

Buddy   Genre?

Guy   Political thriller. Hailed as −

Buddy   Logline.

Guy   Christian right and young Islam make peace on the run. Fundamentalism finds a middle ground.

Buddy   Jesus.

Guy   With jokes. And don't say Jesus.

Buddy   Where's it end?

Guy   Ground Zero. New York's finest.

Buddy   Buzz.

Guy   Sensitive but accessible. Multiplex *Kane* of its generation.

Buddy   My generation, Guy, my generation. Let's go. Get him up here.

Guy *picks up the phone and punches a button.*

Guy (*into phone*)   Could you send Mr Faruk up, please?

Buddy   Good. Now, when he arrives, keep him waiting for seventy-five seconds, OK?

Guy   OK. (*Beat.*) I'm excited.

Buddy   It's all a dream, Guy.

Guy   What?

Buddy   It's all a dream. Just roll with it, OK?

Guy   OK. What are you going to say?

Buddy   Whatever he wants to hear. Remember, seventy-five seconds.

Guy   OK.

Buddy *heads into his office, frosting the windows. Pause.* **Daniel** *enters warily. He is sleekly attractive and genuinely passionate, but makes the presumptions of an ingénue who is beginning to believe his own hype.*

Guy   Mr Faruk.

Daniel   Guy?

Guy   Hello.

Daniel   This was your idea.

Guy   Well, I –

Daniel   Well, get your hopes down, OK? I'm not happy about this.

Guy   I understand, just listen to what he has to say.

Daniel   Where is he?

Guy   He's on a call.

Daniel   I'm not waiting for him to finish his goddamn conversation, Guy, I'm here now.

Guy   I –

Daniel   He's pitching to me.

Guy   I know.

Daniel   An' what he has to say better be pretty damn special, man. My time is important.

Guy   Of course.

Daniel   An' not just to me. To the cinemagoing re-public. He oughta count himself lucky. (*Beat.*) Feel like I'm in a fuckin' KKK meetin' here. Dealin' with the devil.

Guy   He'll just be another few seconds, I promise.

Beat.

Daniel   You really think Buddy can make this?

Guy   He can make it, sure.

Daniel   But can he make it right? No stars, no sequels, no nothin'?

Guy   He said –

Daniel   I don't care what he said. What do you think?

Beat.

Guy   I give you my word, Daniel. You go with Buddy on this and I will personally ensure your vision gets the treatment it deserves.

Beat. **Guy** *looks to* **Buddy**'s *office.*

Daniel   Only reason I'm here, Dawn Lockard.

Guy   Really.

Daniel   Hell, yeah. She is a kind lady.

Guy   Yes, she is.

Daniel   Kind to me. (*Beat.*) You know, she told me about you.

Guy   Really?

Daniel   Yeah. Coupla nights back. We had some champagne. Her place. (*Beat.*) An' she just kept talking about you.

Guy   What did she say?

Daniel   She said –

Buddy *opens the door to his office.*

Buddy   Daniel.

Daniel   Mr Ackerman.

Buddy   Buddy, please.

Buddy *approaches and offers his hand.* **Daniel** *takes it and shakes it once.*

Daniel   I want you to be aware that this is a very special project.

Buddy   Oh, I know.

Daniel   The likes of which has never graced a studio of your particular quality.

Buddy   That's why we're here, Dan.

Daniel   That's why you're here, Mr Ackerman.

Buddy   You know what? You're right. (*To* **Guy**.) What the fuck have you done about Andy?

Guy   What?

Buddy   Andy, what the fuck have you done?

Guy   Who's Andy?

Buddy   Did you call his cell?

Guy   I –

Buddy   Did you call his cell?

Beat.

Guy   Yes, I – yes, I left a message.

Buddy   You left a message? (*To* **Daniel**.) Excuse me a minute, Mr Faruk.

Buddy *takes out his cellphone and dials. Pause. The person he is calling answers.*

Buddy (*into phone*)   Andy? Buddy. (*Beat.*) No, listen, I was just checking something, I'll call you back. (*He hangs up.*) Why can I get Andy when you can't?

Guy   I didn't – I –

Buddy   I don't want to hear it, Guy, not again. Get out of my sight.

Guy *turns to go back to his desk.*

Buddy   No, wait, actually, get back here. I want you to hear this.

Guy *stops and turns.*

Buddy   Mr Faruk, do you know anyone who wants to be an assistant? 'Cause I just can't wait to fire this piece of shit.

Guy   Fire me? I –

Buddy (*to* **Daniel**)   Congratulations on *Remuneration*, by the way.

Daniel   You saw that?

Buddy   Through my tears, yes.

Daniel   Thank you, I –

Buddy   That final reel? New York's finest and a union of hearts? Lord above, I wept blood.

Daniel   Really?

Buddy   Really. I am so excited about us working together. Have you eaten?

Daniel   Not yet, no.

Buddy   What do you want?

Daniel   Are you sure? Something healthy.

Buddy   Good, me too. (*To* **Guy**.) Guy, we want two chicken breasts, grilled, no sauce, and a leafy salad with deseeded tomatoes. Bring 'em in in ten.

Guy   But –

Buddy   What now?

Guy   A chicken breast takes twenty minutes.

Buddy   So? Hijack a waiter. (*To* **Daniel**.) After you, Mr Faruk.

Daniel   Thanks, Buddy.

Daniel *enters* **Buddy**'s *office.* **Buddy** *turns to* **Guy**, *smiles and winks.* **Guy**, *confused, sits back down. He stands again and strains to see inside the office. He cannot. Dejected, he picks up the phone and dials.*

Guy (*into phone*)   Hello? (*Beat.*) Yeah, I'd like – I'd like to order some chicken. (*Beat.*) No – grilled, no sauce. And a leafy salad with deseeded tomatoes. (*Beat.*) Ten minutes?

Inside **Buddy**'s *office,* **Buddy** *and* **Daniel** *burst out laughing.* **Guy** *looks toward the laughter and then back again.*

Guy (*into phone*)   No, no – money is no object.

Buddy *opens the door to his office.*

Buddy (*to* **Daniel**)   Hey, I know it sounds grand, but all I want is to bequeath the world something noble, you know?

Daniel (*from inside* **Buddy**'s *office.*)   I do.

Guy *hangs up.*

Buddy (*to* **Guy**)   Scratch the chicken.

Guy   What? I just –

Buddy   We want steaks. And fries. Right? No greens whatsoever. (*Through his door, to* **Daniel**.) Hey, how about a milkshake?

Daniel (*from inside* **Buddy***'s office*)   Are you kidding?

Buddy (*through his door to* **Daniel**)   Thomas's favorite.

Daniel (*from the office*)   Whatever you say.

Buddy (*to* **Guy**)   Two shakes.

Guy (*sotto voce*)   Who's Thomas?

Buddy (*sotto voce*)   My son.

Guy (*sotto voce*)   I didn't know you had a son.

Buddy (*sotto voce*)   He passed away last Christmas.

Guy (*sotto voce*)   Really?

Buddy (*sotto voce*)   No, not really, asshole.

Guy *flinches.*

Daniel (*from the office*)   Come on, Buddy. Let's talk.

Buddy *smiles and looks at* **Guy**.

Buddy   You're on, Guy. Put it together. Let's see what you can do.

Buddy *reenters his office and closes the door.* **Guy** *sits, elated. A soundscape builds recalling the grand, Oscar-winning movies that fuel* **Guy***'s ambition* – Citizen Kane, All Quiet on the Western Front, On the Waterfront, Lawrence of Arabia.

Act Two

Scene One

A bar, six months later. **Guy** *and* **Jack** *sit.* **Jack** *is drinking a mojito.*

Guy   Crews across the globe, locations on three continents, international time zones – the whole shebang. I've been setting this up for six months now, and Daniel Faruk hasn't made a goddamn peep. Does anything I tell him.

Jack   How'd Buddy do it?

Guy   Simple. He satisfied his appetite. First, he got him scared, told him he was alone. Then he told him that, really, they're after the same things, only he upped his expectations. 'Daniel,' he says, 'you want to make a statement so bad, you got to release it to the majors. No war is won through the head-to-head. You really want to beat the enemy, you got to go undercover, put on their clothes.'

Jack   Buddy doesn't believe that.

Guy   What does that matter? He said it. And here we are. Six months down the line and it's, 'Me and you are going to run this place, Guy. We're a team.' He doesn't stop.

Jack   Outstanding.

Guy   I love it, I swear. Working on this, I can feel power flowing through my veins. Actually coursing in the blood. Tomorrow morning, I tell Buddy how the new Daniel Faruk movie could happen. Me.

Jack   You're a hit.

Guy   I'm a success. I swear, I good as run that fuckin' office right now.

Jack   Think you could put in a word?

Guy   Hey, I tell Buddy you're on my team, you're on my team.

Jack   Serious?

Guy   Yeah. I mean, there's paperwork and everything. Time, you know –

Jack   Yeah.

Guy   But it'd happen.

Jack   Great. Do it. (*Beat.*) And how's the chick?

Guy   Good. She's amazing.

Jack   Sounds great.

Guy   I can't sleep unless I'm in her bed, honest to God.

Jack   So when do I meet her?

Guy   I don't know. (*Beat.*) She says she doesn't really want to meet you guys.

Jack   Why not?

Guy   She says you make me seem young. (*Beat.*) It's weird, you know? I thought she trusted me on this. But she won't leave it alone. Like she can't stand me making a decision unless she knows about it a week in advance.

Jack   Sounds tyrannical.

Guy   No, I can handle it. It's just – I keep telling her, this is a big deal for me. For us. And Buddy's not going to listen to her, she knows that. She gets too involved, it'll ruin everything. But still, wherever I turn, there she is. Like, I tell her I have to finish the schedule tonight and she gets pissed.

Jack   You don't want to let her think you're a light touch, Guy. These women, it's your friends close and your enemies naked, with a leash around their fourth finger.

Guy   Dawn's not like that.

Jack   'Sides, breathin' your air, I hear it's good to be unattached.

Guy   Are you kidding me? Buddy's pumping every night, fuckin' chick city. (*Beat.*) Sometimes I look at Dawn, and I think, I'm young, you know? She makes me nervous. (*Beat.*) But no. No, I'm not going to find this again. She's special.

Jack   So is this mojito.

Guy   No, the mojitos here are shit.

Dawn *enters, sees* **Guy**, *and approaches the table.*

Guy   Oh my God.

Jack   What?

Dawn   I knew I'd find you here.

Guy   Hey, what are you doing? I thought –

Dawn *grabs* **Guy** *and kisses him. After a second he pulls away, startled.*

Guy   Jeez. What'd I do?

Dawn   You're like a breeze.

Guy   What?

Dawn   You know, I think I'm getting used to you being so young. You're ten years less complicated than all the other guys I've been with.

Guy   Am I? This is Jack, by the way.

Dawn   The school friend. I'm Dawn.

Jack   Robinson?

Guy   Do you want a drink?

Dawn   No, I won't stay. I just wanted to say thank you.

Guy   Why?

Dawn   I've spent ten years in this town, Guy, and no one's ever bought me flowers.

Guy   Flowers? What flowers?

Dawn What flowers, he says. The flowers in my apartment. That arrived this morning. (*To* **Jack**.) There's hundreds of them.

Beat.

Guy Oh. Yeah.

Dawn (*quietly*) Do you mean it?

Guy (*quietly*) What?

Dawn (*quietly*) What you said in the note.

Beat.

Guy (*quietly*) Yeah. I do.

Dawn (*quietly*) God, I hope you last. (*She kisses him.*) I love you too, Guy. I'll see you tonight, OK?

Guy I told you, I got to work.

Dawn You can do it at my place.

Guy But –

Dawn G'bye, Jack.

Jack (*raising a glass*) Koo-koo ka choo.

Dawn *leaves.* **Guy** *sits. Pause.*

Jack She seems – intense.

Guy Yeah.

Jack Flowers, huh?

Guy Yeah. (*Beat.*) Give me a sip of that.

Scene Two

Keystone, the next morning. **Guy** *enters, tired.* **Buddy** *comes out of his office carrying a thick file.*

Buddy   What time do you call this?

Guy   I was up late.

Buddy   So?

Guy (*indicating the thick file*)   So you wanted it this morning.

Buddy   And I got it this morning. That's not an excuse.

Guy   What were the flowers?

Buddy   Excuse me?

Guy   The flowers. What were they?

Buddy   A gesture.

Guy   Meaning what?

Buddy   Whatever you want. This looks great, by the way. The figures make sense.

Guy   Thank you. Look, how'd you know it was our six-month?

Buddy   You should be grateful.

Guy   That's my personal life, Buddy.

Buddy   Is it?

Guy   Yes.

Buddy   That's strange.

Guy   Why?

Buddy   'Cause you drag her into work every fucking day.

Guy   It's her project.

Buddy   Dawn Lockard has no job here. You've run this show from day one, Guy, and don't think I haven't noticed.

The phone starts ringing. Beat.

You smell of her every morning, you know that? Come in like you've spent the night smothered. Are you going to pick that up?

Guy   I'd appreciate it if –

Buddy   Pick up the phone.

Guy *does so.*

Guy *(into phone)*   Buddy Ackerman's office. *(Beat.)* Hey. *(Beat.)* That's – good. Look, I'm busy, OK? I got to go. *(Beat.)* I – OK. You too.

Guy *hangs up.*

Buddy   You ought to distinguish between work and pleasure, Guy.

Guy   I do.

Buddy   This is business.

Guy   All I mean –

Buddy   Your business. I'm in.

Guy   What? *(Beat.)* Just like that?

Buddy   Just like that. The figures make sense.

Guy   That's great.

Buddy   All's left is the rewrite. Who you got in mind?

Guy   What?

Buddy   We need an expert. Who were you thinking, Monahan? Marber?

Guy   No, no – we agreed no changes.

Buddy   What?

Guy   Those were the conditions, remember? Dawn said we could only have it if there are absolutely no changes.

Buddy   Did she?

Guy   Yeah. She said, she won't trust anyone with this.

Buddy   But –

Guy   No buts. Nothing changes.

Beat.

Buddy   Well, I'm sorry the two of you feel that way.

Buddy *tosses the thick file into a nearby trash can.*

Guy   What are you doing?

Buddy   What does it look like?

Guy   I spent six months on that.

Buddy   It's a piece of shit, Guy, all meaningless with the script as it is.

Guy   That's not true.

Buddy   I can't produce that. It's interesting, sure, but it's not saleable. Cyrus won't get past page ten. Your figures are clouds without a total script overhaul, Guy. Those are your terms, I'm bailing.

Guy   They're not my terms, they're –

Buddy   Bullshit they're not yours, the terms are whatever you want 'em to be. (*Beat.*) Back to work, Guy. Two sugars.

Guy   No.

Buddy   Now.

Guy   No, no, wait. It –

Buddy   What?

Guy   It can work.

Buddy   Oh, really? Let me see. There's no romance. No ending – where's the twist? The structure's as straight as my dick, Guy, sure, but the motivations just don't make any fuckin' sense. There's no drive, no purpose. It's way too depressing.

Guy   But that's life.

Buddy   And this is a movie. Movie life is different. It's simple.

Guy   No.

Buddy   Rosebud. The illusion of two dimensions, Guy, order on chaos. That's the glory of this business. That a man can ride straight into the sunset and not catch fire. 'Cause – kid? The sun only sets if you forget the world is turning. If you're standing still. And that's what a movie has to do. It has to make you, sitting alone in front of a glowing screen, the center of the universe, with the stars spinning just for you, just round your head. A movie makes the sun set for us each alone, Guy. But this – this fuckin' string of scenes – it's just screaming the truth. That we're no more than a slip of chance wheeling for nothing in darkness too empty ever to comprehend. Chaos on order. It's not a movie, it's a cause, and a badly written one at that. This, Guy, this is not my project. I cannot make this.

Guy   I disagree.

Buddy   I wouldn't know where to start.

Guy   I disagree. Granted, it's flawed –

Buddy   It's fucked. We need an expert.

Guy   No, it just needs tweaking.

Buddy   Oh, really? Tweaking. And what tweaks would you propose, wonderboy?

Guy   Well. Look. I agree, the motivations are screwed.

Buddy   Corkscrewed.

Guy   But that just messes up the sense of consequence, not the incidents in themselves. The scenes in isolation are great. It reads like a series of fireworks.

Buddy   So?

Guy   So it's only difficult 'cause it's got no overarching momentum. No throughlines. It's giving too many points equal weight, which denies any sense of teleology, you know? Any satisfaction. Like watching *The Usual Suspects* without a voice-over or Keyser Söze, or *Psycho* without the mother. It's just one shot, then the next, and then it's over. All we need to do is take the penultimate scene – the long one – and cut it up. Stream it throughout the rest of the narrative, plugging the gaps between all the other scenes. That way we boost the inevitability by juxtaposing consequence with cause. We give the whole thing coherence without fucking up the scenes themselves.

Beat.

Buddy   Go on.

Guy   Well, what else is there? The romance is easy. The reason it's unengaging is because the characters don't have any choice. The girl's gold-hearted, and the guy – they're both just instruments of the writer, of his formula, not of themselves. They're jackhammered into the plot instead of its motivating factors. Give them agency, give them choice, and it'll come alive.

Beat.

Buddy   So at the end he –

Guy   No. At the end you reverse it. Take the agency away. Because by then the movie's established its own sense of fate. No matter how downbeat the close, it'll play so long as he's chosen his path to choicelessness, trust me.

Beat.

Buddy   How long would this take?

Guy   What?

Buddy   To fix. How long?

Guy   I don't know. No time, you found the right guy.

Buddy   A week?

Guy   Sure. (*Beat.*) But this is all academic, Buddy. Dawn won't let anyone touch this. I won't let anyone touch this.

Beat.

Buddy   She'd let you.

Guy   What? No, she wouldn't.

Buddy   But if you called it, she wouldn't have a choice.

Guy   I'm not going to call it.

Buddy   You want to be a writer, Guy?

Guy   Yeah.

Buddy   Then write.

Guy   Me?

Buddy   Yeah. You think you could make this work?

Guy   Yes, but Dawn won't –

Buddy   It's your project.

Guy   It's our project.

Buddy   You make this work, it goes straight to Cyrus.

Guy   Cyrus?

Buddy   Sure. With your name on it. Your credit.

Guy   What credit?

Buddy   Co-producer.

Guy   But –

Buddy   All right, executive producer. Three-, four-picture deal, Guy, minimum. You'll be a star, assistant made good. You've heard those stories, right? Right place, right time.

Guy   Sure, but –

Buddy   Well, this is it. Here. Right now.

Guy   But Dawn –

Buddy   You think it's a better script with these changes? With your changes?

Guy   Yes.

Buddy   Then why wouldn't Dawn let 'em through?

Guy   Because she's principled, Buddy.

Buddy   Principled my ass. I'll tell you why. Because Dawn Lockard doesn't trust anything she can't control. She can't beat. (*Beat.*) Look, Guy, you think she's going to let you take credit on her movie?

Guy   Yeah, I do.

Buddy   You just watch her when you suggest this. You just watch. It's going to be her way or no way, mark my words, Guy. I, on the other hand, am giving you freedom. I am giving you artistic license. I have faith in you. The rewrite is yours or the project dies.

Guy   What about Daniel?

Buddy   What about him?

Guy   He won't agree anything without Dawn. She brought us the job.

Buddy   So? Talk to him. Tell him what you told me.

Guy   No, he's her guy. I can't talk to Daniel unless Dawn –

Buddy   What? Unless she what? What makes them so fuckin' close? (*Beat.*) You know how many wet-eyed hopefuls would bury their mothers for this opportunity? Huh? I am on your side. She is not. I want to take this to Cyrus. She wants Stella. You could be a god. You will be a fuckin' eunuch, choking your last as your girlfriend sweeps the awards that should've been yours. Are you going to let her take credit for your work, Guy? Is that what you want?

Guy   No.

Buddy   Can I be more clear?

Guy   No. No.

Buddy   So, go to work, Shakespeare. Make it yours. You have one week.

Buddy *holds out the file. Pause.* **Guy** *takes it.*

Guy   I'll talk to Dawn.

Buddy   Yes, you will.

Scene Three

Dawn*'s apartment.*

Dawn   No, Guy, no fucking way. I let you have this because we were –

Guy   You let me have this?

Dawn   Yes, I let you. I let you in on this because you promised. Because you promised me, Guy.

Guy   Oh, so what?

Dawn   So what?

Guy   That's just what people say. It doesn't mean anything unless –

Dawn   Unless what? Unless it's on paper? You want to contract me?

Guy   You're being childish. It's a couple of changes.

Dawn   A couple? It's the ending, Guy. (*She hits him.*) It's the fucking structure. (*She hits him again.*) You're screwing up the whole message. How's this film going to make a difference –

*As **Dawn** makes to hit **Guy** again, he grabs her arms and pins them by her side.*

Guy   What movie ever made a difference?

Dawn   This is my work.

Guy   Our work. I put it together.

Dawn So?

Guy So you wouldn't have anything if it wasn't for me.

Dawn I'd have Stella.

Guy Yeah, well, not anymore.

Beat.

Dawn Let go of me.

Guy Are you going to hit me again?

Dawn It hurts.

He lets her go.

I say no changes, Guy.

Guy It's not your call.

Dawn Oh, really? I tell Daniel you're trying to fuck with the script –

Guy I already talked to Daniel.

Dawn What?

Guy I already talked to him. Told him the changes. (*Beat.*) He agreed them, Dawn. He thinks they're great. (*Beat.*) Daniel's with me on this now. With Buddy. And Stella's gonna be gone in a month, you know that. It's this way or no way, Dawn. (*Beat.*) Look, the changes'll make it better.

Dawn How?

Guy They'll cover over the cracks, make it easier to watch. People won't have to question it so much.

Dawn The point is that people question it.

Guy The point is that people watch it, Dawn.

Pause.

Dawn Fine.

Guy What?

Dawn   Take it. It's in your hands.

Guy   Thank you.

Dawn   But no changes are being made in my name.

Guy   What? You're ditching your credit?

Dawn   No. The credit stays. But that's it. If the script shifts, I don't want anything else to do with it. Not on the set, not in post, not at the screening, nothing. (*Beat.*) Even if that includes you.

Guy   You're being ridiculous.

Dawn   It's your call, Guy. Me or him.

Beat.

Guy   I want both.

Dawn   I told you when we started this.

Guy   I made a commitment.

Dawn   You think that means something to him?

Beat.

Guy   Don't.

Dawn   Why not?

Guy   Because you're – you're what I look forward to. You're the only real thing I have.

Dawn   Then give up the movie.

Pause. **Guy** *is inert.*

Dawn   You don't want me, Guy. Just get out.

Guy   Fine. You're not in charge anymore, you bail. All this fuckin' preaching, you can't actually handle it, can you?

Dawn   What?

Guy   Being equal.

Dawn   There's no such thing

Guy   You told it to me, Dawn. You got to give action to get action. You're not exempt just 'cause you got a pair of tits.

Pause.

Dawn   Congratulations, Guy. You just graduated. You're going to make a killing in this business. Now fuck off.

Guy *leaves. The romantic soundscape which built at the end of Act One, Scene Three plays, gradually mixed with the soundscape of the classics from the end of Scene Eight. The clash gradually distorts to an iconoclastic babel that crackles with the manic backstage noises of a studio set. This builds in fervor as the scenery and lighting shift from* **Dawn***'s apartment to the office of the next scene. The soundscape perhaps climaxes with the loud toll of a bell marking silence for the beginning of a take.*

Scene Four

Keystone. **Buddy** *sits in his office flicking through a script, laughing.* **Guy** *stands at the foot of* **Buddy***'s desk, haggard and serious.*

Buddy   This is genius, sheer, cold, cruel fucking genius. It sings, it flies of the page. How did you – how did you do this? You did this in a week?

Guy   I haven't been sleeping.

Buddy   I read it twice. This is great work, Guy.

Guy   Well, you said you needed an ending.

Buddy   But that twist, it's real, it's believable. It makes sense.

Guy   It's his life or his love, you know? What's more noble than that?

Buddy   No, absolutely. Absolutely. He's a real hero now.

Guy   Yeah.

Buddy   I tell you, kid, it is say goodbye Stella, hello Buddy and Guy. This is gonna be the best meal of my life.

Guy   What do you mean?

Buddy   I mean lunch. I mean Cyrus, the club, right now.

Guy   What?

Buddy   I gave it to him this morning, Guy. Two hours later we're summoned to eat. I feel an announcement coming. I feel a celebration.

Guy   That's – you gave it to Cyrus already? Thank you, Buddy. That's –

Buddy   No, no – thank you. You did it, Guy. Congratulations. Click your fingers. Go on.

Guy *does.*

Buddy   The world just changed.

Guy   Wow.

Buddy   You deserve it.

Guy   I'd better get dressed.

Buddy   What?

Guy   I've been wearing these clothes all night. The club? I need to change.

Buddy   What do you mean?

Guy   For lunch. I'm not dressed.

Buddy   No. You're not coming.

Guy   What?

Buddy   You're not coming. (*Beat.*) We don't want to crowd him, Guy. I've got to do this alone.

Guy   But – it's my project.

Buddy   The Pooh-Bah's old. He doesn't trust new sources, OK? It has to be seen as coming from me first, at least at this stage. It's attrition. I feed him a new little tidbit every day, work you into his consciousness. It's the only way to do this.

Guy But I –

Buddy You don't want to drop the ball now, do you? When you've come all this way?

Guy No.

Buddy So you give it to me to touch down. We're on the same team, Guy. We both win.

Guy But –

Buddy But nothing. You wait and see.

Buddy *picks up a windup toy, winds it up, and sets it in motion on his desk. Beat.*

Guy OK.

Buddy Now, look. Daniel's waiting for me outside. Would you mind telling him to hold two minutes? I need to freshen up.

Guy No. (*Beat.*) No, not at all.

Buddy Thank you. You're a prince, Guy. One in a million.

Guy *exits.* **Buddy** *watches the toy walk toward the edge of the desk. He catches it just before it falls to the floor and smiles to himself. He then moves to the door of his office, takes out his cellphone and, without dialing, begins to talk into it, moving back into his office.*

Buddy (*ostensibly into the cellphone*)   I couldn't be happier, Cap'n.

Guy *reenters and moves to the doorway of* **Buddy**'s *office.*

Guy He wasn't –

Buddy *covers the cellphone mouthpiece.*

Buddy Cyrus. (*Ostensibly into cellphone.*) Daniel's with you already? He was just outside. (*Beat.*) No – no sweat. You'll love him, he's great. (*Beat.*) A hundred million bucks great, low end. That's how great. Though I gotta tell you, where we'd be without Guy, I don't even – (*Beat.*) Guy? Oh, he is fan-fuckin'-tastic. He's the best. The best I've ever had. (*Beat.*) Are you kidding? I'm gonna have to start watching my back.

Guy *smiles. The phone on his desk rings. He moves to the desk and picks up the phone.*

Guy (*into phone*)   Buddy Ackerman's office.

Buddy (*ostensibly into cellphone*)   Bona fide wonderboy, I'm telling you.

Guy (*into phone*)   Cyrus? I'm sorry – Mr Miles? But – (*Beat.*) No, no, I'm sorry, I just – (*Beat.*) You're looking for – (*Beat.*) For Buddy. Of course.

Buddy *appears in his doorway, beaming.*

Buddy (*ostensibly into cellphone*)   No, the rewrite was all Guy.

Guy (*into phone*)   He's on the other line, I'm afraid.

Buddy (*ostensibly into cellphone*)   He just ran with it.

Guy (*into phone*)   My name?

Buddy (*ostensibly into cellphone*)   Genius, I'm tellin' you. You think I could write like that?

Guy (*into phone*)   My name is Guy, sir.

Buddy (*ostensibly into cellphone*)   He's the one to watch.

Guy (*into phone*)   My name is Guy.

Guy *hangs up.*

Buddy (*ostensibly into cellphone*)   The shooting star. (*He makes a 'thumbs-up' gesture at* **Guy**.) Uh-huh. (*Beat.*) OK. Yeah. I'll be twenty minutes. (*Beat.*) Bye-bye. (*He hangs up and pockets his cellphone.*) Who was that?

Guy   It was personal.

Buddy   I've told you before, no personals.

Guy   I'm sorry.

Beat.

Buddy   You see, Guy? I'm looking out for you. Listen to me, nobody else. Because I have your best interests at heart. (*Beat.*) In fact, you know what?

Guy What?

Buddy   I want you to take the rest of the day off. I'm going to celebrate, you should too. (*He takes out his wallet and gives* **Guy** *a wad of bills.*) Take this. I want you out. Out on the town, OK? Report back tomorrow morning. And it better be wild.

Guy Thank you.

Buddy No, thank you. You deserve this.

Guy I guess I do.

Buddy Now scram.

Guy OK. Thank you.

Guy *leaves, cash in hand.* **Buddy** *watches him go. He then picks up* **Guy***'s desk phone and dials. Lights up on* **Dawn***, alone in her apartment. The phone rings. She looks at the phone to check the incoming number, hesitates, and picks up.*

Dawn (*into phone*) Guy?

Buddy (*into phone*) Oh. I'm sorry, Dawn, it's me. I'm actually looking for Guy, though. Have you seen him?

Dawn (*into phone*) No. I haven't seen him in a while, actually.

Buddy (*into phone*) Oh, that's right, I forgot. Sorry.

Dawn (*into phone*) That's OK.

Buddy (*into phone*) Listen, I've been meaning to say, I haven't forgot who brought me *Arab Redemption*.

Dawn (*into phone*) Arab what?

Buddy (*into phone*) New title. Guy's, actually. Kid's a genius. But I haven't forgotten who brought it to me in the first place. I'm grateful. (*Beat.*) So, anyway. I was wondering whether you might want to discuss your credit. As co-producer.

Dawn (*into phone*) Co?

Buddy (*into phone*) Sure. You and Guy. How's tonight?

Beat.

Dawn (*into phone*)   You're not really looking for Guy, are you, Buddy?

Buddy (*into phone*)   Oops. You caught me. What do you say?

Dawn (*into phone*)   I'd say I'm really busy. Sorry.

Buddy (*into phone*)   You forgetting what I taught you? Never apologize, it's a –

Dawn (*into phone*)   Sign of weakness. Never forgot it.

Buddy (*into phone*)   You know, I can remember the days when, faced with an opportunity like this from anyone else, you would've scurried over like an eager beaver.

Dawn (*into phone*)   Yeah, well, those days are long gone.

Buddy (*into phone*)   And your career has been on hold.

Dawn (*into phone*)   I got to go, Bud—

Buddy (*into phone*)   It's Guy, isn't it? What's wrong? Can't see the boss 'cause you're too busy mourning the assistant?

Dawn (*into phone*)   Yeah, that's it. That's it exactly.

Buddy (*into phone*)   Fine. He's no longer the assistant.

Dawn (*into phone*)   Excuse me?

Buddy (*into phone*)   You heard. He's history, he's gone. There. Any problems coming over now?

Dawn (*into phone*)   Guy is not the problem, Buddy.

Buddy (*into phone*)   Well, maybe he is and maybe he isn't, but there's really only one way to find out now, isn't there?

Dawn (*into phone*)   Fuck you.

Buddy (*into phone*)   Come on. It's just another night. Another long, lonely night. (*Beat.*) I don't see what the big deal is. You were basically fucking me all along.

Dawn (*into phone*)   What do you mean?

Buddy (*into phone*)   Oh, please. The whole relationship was strategic, Dawn. It was all part of the takeover. Soon as I explained what you could do for him, he did anything I asked.

Dawn (*into phone*)   Bullshit.

Buddy (*into phone*)   His big break, we called it. Christ, he got so involved I thought he was going to propose. I mean, the flowers? Come on.

Dawn (*into phone*)   How do you know about the flowers?

Buddy (*into phone*)   How do you think? (*Beat.*) You know what he's like. Underneath that seal-cub naivety there's a fuckin' shark. You were useful. (*Beat.*) And now you're going to stall your career over that piece of shit? Christ. There's atoning for your sins, Dawn, and there's plain fucking stupidity. (*Beat.*) Come on. I make President, you're my number two. How about it?

Dawn (*into phone*)   What do you mean?

Buddy (*into phone*)   I mean it's you or him, Dawn. If I tell Cyrus that you brought me the movie –

Dawn (*into phone*)   What do you mean, 'make President'?

Beat.

Buddy (*into phone*)   Well. When Cyrus sees *Arab*, he won't have a choice.

Beat.

Dawn (*into phone*)   Your number two, huh?

Buddy (*into phone*)   My place. Midnight. And it's yours. (*Beat.*) It's been a long time coming, Dawn.

Pause.

Dawn (*into phone*)   Fuck you.

She hangs up. **Buddy** *smiles and hangs up.*

Scene Five

Bar, that night. **Guy** *sits with* **Jack**. *Both are drunk. A bottle of champagne is on the table and other, empty, bottles are upended in a nearby cooler.* **Guy** *fills* **Jack**'s *champagne flute and then swigs from the bottle.*

Guy   This fuckin' world, Jack, you don't understand. You don't understand it.

Jack   Sure I do.

Guy   No you don't, you –

Daniel *passes them while walking toward the exit.* **Jack** *notices him.*

Jack   Oh shit, Guy, Guy, it's Daniel Faruk. Introduce us, that man is my god.

Daniel *sees* **Guy** *and approaches the table.*

Daniel   Guy. They let you out of the salt mine.

Guy   To keep an eye on you, Daniel.

Daniel *and* **Jack** *laugh.*

Jack   To keep an eye –

Guy   Daniel, this is Jack. He's interning at Paramount.

Daniel   Good for you.

Jack   You're very meaningful.

Daniel   Thank you.

Jack   Absolutely one of the best.

Daniel (*to* **Guy**)   How's Buddy?

Guy   Exceptional.

Daniel   You're tellin' me. His rewrite, man. That guy's got talent.

Guy   He can pick 'em.

Jack   Buddy's rewrite?

Guy   That's just what people say.

Daniel   Breakin' up that scene and streamin' it through? Best thing I ever read.

Guy   Yeah.

Daniel   Anyway. Good seein' you.

Guy   Daniel.

Jack   Great to meet you.

Daniel *moves to the exit.*

Jack   God. Daniel Faruk. What a cool guy.

Guy   He's an idiot, Jack.

Jack   What?

Daniel *passes* **Mitzy** *in the entrance.* **Mitzy** *mistakes him for a waiter, hands him her coat, and walks on.* **Daniel** *drops the coat on the floor and exits.*

Guy   They're all fucking idiots.

Jack   I know.

Guy   We used to be kids, for God's sake. Everything was – clean. Look at us. I can't even remember what it looks like outdoors.

Jack   It's just out there.

Mitzy *recognizes* **Guy** *and approaches the table.*

Mitzy (*Valley Girl voice*)   Guy, hi, you look so well.

Guy *shoots to his feet, knocking over the cooler.*

Guy   For fuck's sake, stop.

Bottles roll over the floor. No one bats an eyelid.

Mitzy   How've you been?

Guy   What?

Mitzy   You look so tan. Have you been working out?

Guy   I'm pale, Mona –

Mitzy   Mitzy.

Guy   Oh, grow up. I'm pale. I look like shit.

Mitzy *laughs.*

Mitzy   You're so funny, Guy.

Guy   How do you know my name?

Mitzy   Excuse me?

Guy   I never introduced myself to you.

Mitzy   Everyone knows your name, Guy. We all know who you are. Though I shouldn't be talking to you.

Guy   Why not?

Mitzy   Buddy stopped returning my calls, Guy. I should be mad.

Guy   I –

Mitzy   But I might consider forgiving you, if you got me another meeting.

Guy   No.

Mitzy   Come on, Guy. I'm not poisonous.

Guy   I can't.

Mitzy   I'd make it worth your while.

Guy   Where'd you go to school?

Mitzy   What?

Guy   Where did you go to school?

Mitzy   Stanford.

Beat.

Guy   I'm sorry. You've got to go. I'm sorry.

Jack   I'm Jack, by the way.

Mitzy   What do you do?

Jack   I'm – uh – I'm over at Paramount.

Mitzy   What position?

Jack   Intern.

Beat.

Mitzy   Cool. (*Beat.*) Smoke?

Jack   Of course.

Jack *stands and exits with* **Mitzy**. **Guy** *is left alone. He takes out his cellphone and dials.*

Lights up on **Dawn**, *alone in her apartment. The phone is ringing.* **Dawn** *looks at the caller ID and picks up.*

Dawn (*into phone*)   Hello?

Guy (*into phone*)   Dawn? Dawn, it's me.

Dawn (*into phone*)   Oh. Hi.

Beat.

Guy (*into phone*)   It's good to hear your voice. You sound real.

Dawn (*into phone*)   Are you drunk?

Guy (*into phone*)   No. (*Beat.*) A little. (*Beat.*) How've you been?

Dawn (*into phone*)   OK. (*Beat.*) You?

Guy (*into phone*)   I need to talk to you.

Dawn (*into phone*)   What about?

Guy (*into phone*)   I'll explain, just – I miss you, and I want to see you. Please. I just really want to talk to you. (*Beat.*) I'm sorry, Dawn. You were right. I want out. I'll leave Buddy. I can do it, I swear. I just want you.

Beat.

Dawn (*into phone*)   Were the flowers your idea?

Guy (*into phone*)   What?

Dawn (*into phone*)   The flowers. Were they your idea?

Beat.

Guy (*into phone*)   It's just a fucking detail. Please. Let me come over.

Dawn (*into phone*)   No.

Guy (*into phone*)   Why not?

Dawn (*into phone*)   I'm busy.

Guy (*into phone*)   What, are you seeing someone? A man?

Dawn (*into phone*)   A man. You know what, Guy? That's a good idea. Because I'm sick of playing with little children.

Guy (*into phone*)   I'm not –

Dawn (*into phone*)   You lied to me, Guy.

Guy (*into phone*)   What?

Dawn (*into phone*)   I know about Buddy.

Guy (*into phone*)   What about him?

Dawn (*into phone*)   Christ, you are a child. (*Beat.*) I know he's not President of Production, Guy.

Guy (*into phone*)   What are you talking about?

Dawn (*into phone*)   I know what you've both been doing.

Guy (*into phone*)   I haven't been doing anything. He's not President?

Dawn (*into phone*)   Goodbye, Guy.

Guy (*into phone*)   Wait.

Dawn (*into phone*)   What?

Beat.

Guy (*into phone*)   I love you, Dawn. I love you. Please – I – I didn't know. It's just – talk without you. Pictures. Please. I love you.

Beat.

Dawn (*into phone*)   I don't believe you.

Guy (*into phone*)   I just want to do what's right.

Dawn (*into phone*)   No. You want it done for you. Goodbye, Guy.

Dawn *hangs up. Beat.* **Guy** *looks around him. Outside,* **Mitzy** *laughs.* **Guy** *puts his phone on the table, staring at it. He stands, unnervingly calm, and leaves.*

Scene Six

The poolside terrace of **Buddy**'s *lavish, masculine apartment in the remote Hollywood Hills. While immediately impressive, the decor is unsettlingly severe.*

Sliding glass doors lead inside, where a door leads to a kitchen, unseen. Outside, there is an iPod music system, an exercise machine and a small table bearing trade magazines, a phone dock, and a clock.

Buddy *walks through the open sliding doors, dressed in workout clothes and speaking on his wireless house phone.*

Buddy (*into phone*)   Guy, listen, my sofa's all wrong, I can't even look at it. Tomorrow morning I want you to go to Rodeo Drive and take a camera. I want a photo of every sofa in every shop. Top priority, Guy, don't fuck it up.

A door opens somewhere offstage. **Buddy** *turns toward the noise with the phone to his ear, but dismisses it.*

And colour-code the photos. Light to dark.

He hangs up and looks out over the hills. Long pause. He presses speed-dial and raises the phone to his ear. The call goes straight to answerphone.

After you fix the sofa, research the director of the new Def Jux promo. It's got this blonde. She's wearing this, um, this like American flag . . . kind of . . . gym thing on her ass. It's – scratch that, it may just be they've painted her ass. Um . . . I don't know . . . set up a meeting. She's . . . She's really . . . She's talented.

Buddy *hangs up the phone in the dock on the table. Pause. He sits down on the exercise machine and begins working out.*

Guy *steps out of the shadows into the light. He is carrying a large bag and a near-empty whiskey bottle.*

Guy   The video was directed by a she.

Buddy *(spinning round and standing)*   What the hell?

Guy *drops the bag.*

Guy   Tracy Janawitz. And you're a little late, she just signed a three-picture deal with Paramount.

Buddy   What the fuck –

Guy   And as far as the blonde –

He pours the remainder of the whiskey onto the floor and then drops the bottle.

Buddy   What are you doing?

Guy   Don't you think she's a little young? Even for you?

Buddy   What are you doing here? Jesus Christ, you scared the living shit out of me. You're lucky I didn't shoot you.

Guy   With what, this?

Guy *pulls a gun from his belt. Beat.*

Buddy   Oh, great, my gun. Hand it over.

Guy   Sit.

Buddy   Have you gone completely insane? Give me the gun now.

Guy *upturns the table, throwing the trades and the clock to the floor. He points the gun.*

Guy   Sit the fuck down now.

Buddy *sits. Beat.*

Buddy   OK, look, I know things have been a little crazy lately but there's no need for this. Now, why don't you put down the gun and let's talk. We're both rational adults here.

Guy   Bullshit. You are a fucking child.

The phone rings. **Buddy** *and* **Guy** *look toward it. Beat.* **Buddy** *makes a dash for the phone.* **Guy** *shoots it, shattering its plastic shell.*

Guy   Sit.

Buddy *sits.*

Buddy   What do you want?

Guy   I want you to think, and remember every insult, every offense. I want you to imagine every life-shielding dream that you have taken away from me. And I want you to think to yourself, it's payback time. Payback, remember?

Buddy   I'll give you –

Guy   There's nothing.

Over the ensuing lines, **Guy** *takes duct tape out of his bag and ties* **Buddy** *to the exercise machine. He then takes* **Buddy**'s *cellphone out of his pocket.*

Buddy   That's a lie. You want something.

Guy   Nope.

Buddy   Partnership.

Guy   You already gave me that. Remember?

Buddy   Money. Pussy.

Guy *cocks the gun.*

Buddy   You are in big trouble, Guy. I swear, big trouble, if you don't let me go right now. You better start making funeral arrangements, kid, because if you don't let me go you are dead in this town, I am not kidding you.

Guy *chuckles.*

Buddy   What's so funny?

Guy   You're right. I probably will have to make funeral arrangements. For you. No one else'll give a fuck, that'll be my job. Don't you think that's funny?

Beat.

Buddy   Are you going to kill me?

Guy   Yeah. (*Beat.*) But not yet. First –

Buddy   What?

Guy   You're going to apologize.

Buddy   Excuse me? What?

Guy *yanks* **Buddy***'s hair.*

Buddy   Ow, ow, my hair!

Guy   Apologize.

Buddy   Fuck you. What've I got to be sorry for?

Guy *punches* **Buddy** *in the face several times. He then reels, holding his hands.*

Guy   Jesus Christ, that hurts. Christ. I thought people just keep going.

Buddy (*yelling*)   Help! Help! Help! Help!

Pause.

Guy   Are you done?

Buddy   I can't apologize until I know what I'm apologizing for.

Guy   You want to know?

Buddy   Yes.

Guy   You really want to know?

Buddy   Yes.

Beat.

Guy   You're going to regret saying that, Buddy.

Buddy   Why?

Guy *moves to the stereo and scrolls through the music.*

Guy   Let me ask your opinion on something. 'Cause I'd consider you something of an expert on the subject. What is the best getting-laid music? I mean, I've got loads of R&B, Marvin Gaye, all that stuff, but it's just – I never feel I can live up to it, you know? All that fuckin' whispering and I'm still fumbling for a zip. What's your favorite?

Buddy   Fuck you.

Guy   I always imagined I was going to start by cutting off your dick. It's strange, I'm straight, never questioned it. But the number of times I've fantasized about cutting off your dick – about making you know how it feels, in these last hours of your miserable fuckin' life. How it feels to be half a man. (*Beat.*) But now that I'm here, I think I'm going to save that for later. Start slow and build up, you know? Give it the right structure. After all, I don't want you to bleed to death. (*He finds a tune.*) Ah, perfect.

He presses 'play' on the stereo. The first movement of Vivaldi's Winter Concerto, Op. 8, No. 4, RV 297, from The Four Seasons *plays.*

Aren't associations funny? I heard this all the time as a kid, and it was peaceful to me. But then I saw *Old Boy.* Remember? When he rips the guy's teeth out with a hammer? Korean, I didn't understand a fuckin' word, but the hammer scene . . . Now, I can't listen to this without wanting to tear something apart.

Buddy   I'll give you whatever you want.

Guy   I want you to be sorry. (*Beat.*) Where to begin, where to begin.

Guy *opens his bag and begins to take out a series of commonplace but sinister household appliances.* **Buddy** *sees this and cranes around to look at the clock on the floor.*

Buddy (*quietly*)   Fuck. Fuck. Please, please. (*To* **Guy**.) You haven't thought this through at all, have you? You kill me, you go to prison the rest of your life.

Guy   Really? They'll pick me out of all the starlet crazies you cheat each night? Please. City's a fuckin' museum of them. 'I don't know, officer. It was a revolving door. They all knew where the key was.' Cops'll give up in a week.

Beat.

Buddy   You won't do it.

Guy   Why not?

Buddy   You don't have what it takes. And you know it, Guy. Why don't you just let me go, huh? And we'll forget all about it.

Guy   I don't have what it takes. Really. (*He finds something in his bag.*) Oh yes. Perfect.

Guy *takes the item from his bag and hides it behind his back. He approaches* **Buddy**.

Buddy   Stay away from me.

Guy   What are you going to do, bite me? (*Beat.*) It's funny. I only really dreamt about doing all these things. All those lonely nights in the office. Those weekends. Playing out these torture scenarios in my head, over and over and over again. You can't imagine what I've come up with.

He stands behind **Buddy**.

Buddy   Whatever you're thinking of doing, please don't.

Guy   Shhh.

Guy *theatrically produces an envelope and holds it in front of* **Buddy**. **Buddy** *breathes relief.* **Guy** *sharply pulls the envelope taut a couple of times, making a cracking noise.*

Guy   Paper cuts. Now they can be a bitch. Occupational hazard, I guess. But I bet it's been a while since you had one, huh? Me, I'm starting to get used to 'em.

Guy *gently tilts* **Buddy**'s *chair back, holds his head and slowly runs the envelope's fold across* **Buddy**'s *cheek, leaving a thin trail of blood.*

Buddy   Oh – God –

Guy *takes the envelope away.* **Buddy** *gasps, breathless.*

Guy   Stings, doesn't it? Well, like I said, you'll get used to 'em.

He cuts **Buddy** *twice more on the face.*

Buddy   Jesus – Christ –

Guy *surveys his handiwork.*

Guy   Pretty. Really. But you know what? You know the ones that I could never handle? (*He viciously grabs* **Buddy**'s *cheeks with one hand and squeezes.*) Say 'Ah'. Come on. You're only going to make it harder on yourself. (*Beat.*) Forget about the shitty mint flavor on these things. The real pain in the ass is when you get a paper cut on your tongue.

Buddy (*muffled*)   No –

His protests are cut off as **Guy** *forces his mouth open.* **Guy** *moves in.* **Buddy** *screams, muffled.* **Guy** *finishes and blood trickles out of* **Buddy**'s *mouth. He begins to cry.*

Buddy   What do you want? You sick twisted fuck. Why are you doing this? This – this isn't going to fix things. This isn't going to help any of your problems.

Guy   You know, you're right. But it makes me feel so much better.

Buddy   Fuck you. A couple of cuts and you go postal. You whiny fuckin' crybaby.

Guy   This isn't about me.

Buddy   Bullshit.

Guy   I'm teaching you a lesson. I'm making you a fucking lesson. Because next week, all over this town, people like you are going to pick up the trades and see pictures of your broken body. And they're going to be afraid. Because it's their turn.

Buddy   Turn?

Guy   Your turn to feel how you treat people. To feel it's wrong.

Buddy   I haven't done anything wrong.

Guy   What else? (*He rummages in his bag again.*) Oh, God, that is perfect.

He begins to take bottles out of the bag. **Buddy** *struggles against his bonds helplessly.*

Guy   You know, after you're dead, people are going to remember you. I'll give you that. But what do you think they'll remember you for? What will they write on your gravestone? See, I spend all my nights alone now, so I think a lot about that kind of stuff. The morbid side of things. You know what I think they'll write?

Buddy   No.

Guy   I think they'll write, 'Here lies Buddy Ackerman. The man who saw the potential in everything.' For example, a cocktail set. It seems ordinary. Harmless, even. But if you isolate the elements – lemon juice, say, or hot sauce – and consider them in a new context, you can make some pretty interesting opportunities. (*He shakes a bottle.*) You know, I saw this in a movie once. Matter of fact, it was one of yours, I think.

He squirts the hot sauce in **Buddy***'s bleeding face.* **Buddy** *screams.*

Guy   What do you think it'll read?

Buddy   My face – wait – please –

Guy   I asked you –

He squirts **Buddy** *again.* **Buddy** *screams again.*

Guy   – what do you think it will read?

Buddy   It's already written.

Guy   What? Really?

Buddy   Elizabeth had it done.

Guy   Elizabeth?

Buddy   My wife, you fucking retard.

Guy   I'd watch your tongue if I were you. (*Beat.*) What's it say?

Beat.

Buddy   'Unreachable'. (*Beat.*) Is this because of Cyrus?

Guy   What?

Buddy   Cyrus, is this –

Guy   Can't you conceive of anything –

Buddy   Listen –

Guy   – outside of your tiny little world?

Buddy   You'll get your credit.

Guy   Executive producer?

Buddy   Yes.

Guy   Because you're President of Production.

Buddy   Yes.

Guy   So you can do that.

Buddy   Yes yes yes.

Guy *squirts* **Buddy** *again.* **Buddy** *screams.*

Guy   Don't lie to me.

Buddy   I'm not lying!

Guy   You're not President.

Buddy   I am! The movie's greenlit, the decision's made.

Guy   When? When was it made?

Beat.

Buddy   Today. (*Beat.*) Cyrus confirmed at lunch.

Guy   Leaving me?

Buddy   Up there with me.

Guy   Bullshit.

Buddy   No, I told Cyrus about you.

Guy   When?

Buddy   On the phone, you heard –

Guy *squirts* **Buddy** *again.* **Buddy** *screams.*

Guy   Do I look that stupid? Do I look that dumb? 'Guy is fan-fucking-tastic.' Unbelievable. Did you really think that you could pull that shit off?

Beat.

Buddy   I'm gonna tell him.

Guy   Bullshit.

Buddy   I am.

Guy   You were going to take credit for everything I did.

Buddy   Oh, you know what? Fuck you, Guy. You gave me no choice.

Guy   What?

Buddy   I did you a fucking favor.

Guy   How?

Buddy   You were getting complacent, Guy, ungrateful.
Complete and total job burnout, and don't think I didn't
notice. You just didn't give a shit anymore, not about the work,
only about your fuckin' credits, your glory.

Guy   I was setting up the movie.

Buddy   But you weren't answering the phones. Dragging
your feet everywhere, telling everybody you were doing my
job, that you were running the show. That without you, I was
nothing. (*Beat.*) Yeah. People tell me things. I didn't let you
think I was going to the top, you wouldn't have lifted a
goddamn finger. And you know what? Then, Guy, you'd still
be pissing in my coffee and crying at your desk. But now look
at you. You're playing in the majors. Or at least, you were,
before this fuckin' stunt. All because of me. So don't come
preaching to me about what I deserve. You're no martyr here,
you're no hero. You're just a fuckin' hypocrite. You're just like
any other punk kid out there looking for a way in, any way in,
so long as it's easy. You need me.

Guy   I don't need you.

Buddy   Bullshit. You need me and you can't stand it. You
see, that's the trouble with your dot-com, *American Idol*, born-
famous fuckin' generation. You all want it now, two minutes
before your twelfth birthday or you're worthless. Well, fuck
you. You think you deserve it just because you want it? It doesn't
work like that. You have to earn it. You have to take it. You
have to make it yours. You know that. I taught you that. Look
at you now.

Guy   I'm not here to take anything, Buddy.

Buddy   Yeah. You're here 'cause you're the sacred fuckin'
avenger. Get real, Guy. I tripped you up 'cause you weren't
running straight, and you deserved it.

Guy   Does that give you the right to belittle me? To abuse
me? Why do you think you have the right –

Buddy   Because I earned it! What, do you think someone just handed me this job? I've handled the phones, I've juggled the bimbos, I've put up with the tyrants, the yellers, the screamers. I've done more than you can even imagine in that small mind of yours. I paid my dues.

Guy   I didn't spend one year –

Buddy   I spent ten! I sacrificed everything I had, damn it, everything – it's my turn to be selfish, it's my turn.

Guy   You're right. It is your turn.

Guy *takes a packet of sugar out of his bag and then heads offstage into the kitchen. We hear water running into a kettle and the kettle being turned on.*

Buddy   Don't run away from this, Guy. You got what you asked for. Please, just let me go. You're not here for me.

Guy (*offstage*)   I'm here because you pander filth to the fucking world.

Buddy   Oh, don't sing yourself to sleep with that horseshit, you little pussy. Righteousness is an excuse, Guy. For people who have to go grand when they lie to themselves or they just won't buy it.

Guy *reemerges.*

Guy   I'm not ashamed of anything. You deserve this.

Buddy   Bullshit.

Guy   It's punishment. It's right.

Buddy   You think you're different?

Guy   Yes.

Buddy   You're the same as everyone else.

Guy   No.

Buddy   Everyone who watches our films –

Guy   Your films.

Buddy   We're all the same. Look at my face.

Guy   You're wrong.

Buddy   Cut the crap, Guy. We're businessmen. We cater to the market, we don't create it.

Guy   A boy in Texas tears out his brother's eye –

Buddy   He would've –

Guy   – with a meat skewer –

Buddy   He would've done it anyway.

Guy   Bullshit.

Buddy   He would have done it anyway but with less style. And you wouldn't have read about it, Guy. Because the headline wasn't 'accident', it was tearing, gouging, socket, jelly, eyeball, pierce, blood, and that's why you read it. That's why you read. (*Beat.*) Not every man has poetry in them, Guy, but every man has violence. Look around you. Awards. Wealth. Fame. It's celebrated. You're standing in a fuckin' temple to it. Why be ashamed? You want it, it could be yours. This proves you, Guy. You're not here because of me.

Guy   I'm here because –

Buddy   What?

Guy   Because I want my life back.

Buddy   What life? I gave you life. Before me you were nothing. Before me you were an inkspot. You want to go back to your miserable, shitty little existence? Go ahead, kill me. You could have left any day. But you stayed. You put up with it. Why? Because without me, you're nothing.

Guy   That's not true.

Buddy   No? Then what else are you?

Guy   I'm –

Buddy   What?

Guy   I'm loved.

Beat. **Buddy** *chuckles.*

Buddy   I can't believe it. That's it? That's why you're doing this? You pussy-whipped little turd.

Guy   Excuse me?

Buddy   This is about Dawn.

Guy   Shut up.

Buddy   Of all the possible reasons why men do anything, the dumbest is always the one. Pussy. All this over a chick? You fool.

Guy   Shut the fuck up.

Buddy   You disappoint me, Guy. You're going to have to start thinking with your head and not your hips. You reckon she's worth all this?

Guy   Yes.

Buddy   Oh, Guy, she's not what you think.

The kettle boils offstage.

Guy   I'd shut the fuck up if I were you.

Buddy   Or you'll what, torture me? Fuck you.

Guy *moves into the kitchen.*

Buddy   She was choking on dick when you were in diapers, Guy.

Guy (*offstage*)   Bullshit.

Buddy   I knew her then, you didn't. That chick was born with a bed on her back and legs spread ready for action −

Guy (*offstage*)   Shut up.

Buddy   Wide as a wind tunnel, Guy, jacked open for any fat-cocked fuckin' exec who needed a little relief. And nothing's changed.

Guy (*offstage*)   What do you know?

Buddy   Christ, Guy, you're young, but you're not an idiot.

Guy *reappears with the kettle.*

Guy   What was that you said to me that first day?

Buddy   Listen to me.

Guy   Sweeteners might as well have fairy dust in them, what you care about is detail?

Buddy   Guy –

Guy   Well, I care about detail too. (*He opens the kettle. Steam billows out.*) The number of burns I've suffered from making you coffee. The scaldings. My hands are bald. I mean, those are bad, they hurt like hell.

He begins to pour the sugar into the steaming kettle.

Buddy   She's not worth it, Guy.

Guy   But here's a little secret. It's worse – so, so much worse – if you've put too much sweetener in. Or sugar. You know why? Because once a heap of sugar has melted into the heat of the water, it sticks to your skin. It stays there, clinging to you at a hundred degrees, eating your flesh like acid glue. The pain lasts about twenty times a normal burn.

Buddy   Please, Guy.

Guy *dips his fingers in the boiling water and recoils in pain.*

Guy   Apologize.

Buddy   She's not what you think.

Guy   Apologize and it's over

Buddy   She was using you.

Guy   Why would she –

Buddy   For the film. To get to me.

Guy   You're lying.

Buddy   I'm not.

Guy   You're lying to me.

Buddy   Come on, Guy. Wake up. Why do you think she's been fucking me?

Guy *pours the water onto* **Buddy***'s knee.* **Buddy** *screams. Over the following lines,* **Guy** *slowly moves the stream of water up* **Buddy***'s leg toward his crotch.*

Guy   Don't say that.

Buddy (*hysterical*)   It's true. She's been fucking me all along. Why do you think I took the project in the first place?

Guy   You're lying.

Buddy (*hysterical*)   Why else would I have taken it? It was always her plan, Guy. The movie was going to put her back on the map, but not without me. Soon as I said no, she needed you. Because she needed me.

Guy   Bullshit.

Buddy (*hysterical*)   When'd she leave? Huh? Soon as the movie was good. Soon as she was set up. She was using you.

Guy *stops pouring the water just before* **Buddy***'s crotch.*

Guy   Don't –

Buddy   I'm not lying, Guy.

Guy   I love her.

Buddy   No, you don't. She's not worth it.

Guy   You don't know what she's worth.

Buddy   Yes I do, I know exactly.

Guy   How?

Buddy   My wife.

Guy   Oh, bullshit. Don't fake a fuckin' heart at me. Look at this place. There isn't a trace of her, not even a picture in the whole goddamn house.

Buddy   Fuck you.

Guy   I bet you didn't even notice she left. What'd she do, run off with another guy? One who gave a shit? What?

Buddy   She died.

Beat.

Guy   My wife died. What a line. (*Beat.*) Was she beautiful?

Buddy   Yes.

Guy   Did you love her?

Buddy   Yes.

Guy   What, then, she get sick of you and end it? Huh? She shoot herself, Buddy? Or did she slice her fuckin' wrists?

Buddy   She was killed.

Guy   What?

Buddy   She was killed, you child. (*Beat.*) You little boy. She was killed. (*Pause.*) Twelve years ago. (*Beat.*) We were married that year. Every week was a new anniversary – three and a half since the first kiss, four years since we met, all of it, the whole schmaltzy business. But the one that was really getting to her was the six-month. After the wedding. She was in a frenzy. I'd been pretending like I didn't care, like I thought she was being sentimental. I had this cheap surprise planned. I was going to pick her up from the mall, take her home, and the place was just going to be heaven – champagne, flowers, the works. I couldn't wait. (*Beat.*) But just as I was leaving work, my boss grabbed me. Told me to type this novel out. The guy had sent in his fuckin' handwritten manuscript, like a thousand pages. I said I couldn't, but – he was going to fire me. (*Beat.*) I kept picturing her face when I told her I'd lost my job. Sitting in all these flowers and hearts. I just couldn't. (*Beat.*) She must've waited for an hour or so, but eventually she caught a lift with this guy who'd been waiting with her. I always said she was too trusting but she just called it being nice. (*Beat.*) He had a couple of friends in the car. They took her to the woods. (*Beat.*) I was at the office till three a.m. banging out this grand fuckin' tragedy, and the whole time I'm thinking, 'Nothing in life is this serious.' I'm thinking, 'Boy, Elizabeth's going to be pissed. When I get home, I'm a dead man.' (*Beat.*) Anyway, I got home, got the message. Went down to the hospital. (*Beat.*) When they were done with her, they just shot her in the head. I saw it, this clean, dark little hole in her temple, and all I could think was, 'That's so – prosaic. Real life.' (*Beat.*) It was a whole week before the police found them – these stupid windup toys she'd bought while she was waiting, and a note. 'In the constant rat race of life, don't ever forget to unwind.' (*Beat.*) She was never really much of a writer.

Beat.

Guy   I didn't know anything about that.

Buddy   Oh, Guy didn't know. Imagine that.

Guy   Hey. That's no excuse for your behavior.

Buddy   You're twenty-four years old, you don't know shit.

Guy   I know what's fair, OK? I know what's right.

Buddy   I can appreciate this. I was young too, felt just like you. Hated authority, hated all my bosses, thought they were full of shit. But listen to me. To do this for Dawn? If you're going to kill me, here's what I know. Here's my legacy. There are no storybook romances. No fairytale endings. Your job is unfair to you? Grow up, way it goes. People use you, life's unfair? Grow up, way it goes. Your girlfriend doesn't love you? Tough shit, way it goes. Your wife gets raped and shot, and they leave their unfinished beers . . . their . . . their stinking longnecks just lying there on the ground? (*Beat.*) So be it. Way it goes. We're all the same, Guy. Selfish like clockwork. And the only dishonesty is to deny it. (*Beat.*) These last months have been the best of your life and you know it. It could carry on like this. We could go to the top, me and you.

Guy   I don't want to.

Buddy   What else could you want?

Guy   Dawn. Just Dawn.

Buddy   Then why'd you steal her project?

Guy   I –

Buddy   I didn't force your hand. Why'd you do the rewrite? Huh? Which was great, Guy, really great. You know I didn't lie about that. You've got it.

Guy   I don't care.

Buddy   She was cheating you.

Guy   I don't believe you.

Buddy   I don't make the rules, I play by them. You don't want an apology, Guy.

Guy   What do I want?

Buddy   You want forgiveness.

Dawn *enters silently through the front door.* **Guy** *does not notice, but* **Buddy** *does. Her hand goes to her mouth to stifle a scream.*

Guy   No. She's different, Buddy. She's better than us.

Buddy   She's worth all this?

Guy   Yes.

Buddy   Because she's pure?

Guy   Yes.

Buddy   Because she loves you?

Guy   Yes. She's the grail, Buddy. She's all there is.

Beat.

Buddy   I would reconsider that statement.

Guy   Why?

Beat.

Buddy   Dawn. Honey. So glad you made it on time, darling, because you got some explaining to do.

Dawn   Guy, what's happening? What are you doing here?

Guy *turns around.*

Guy   No.

Buddy   Now, don't you think that's a question that you should be answering?

Dawn   What? Oh, Christ, no, Guy, this is not what you think.

Buddy   Oh, really? Well, tell us, what are we supposed to think, huh? A young, eager producer comes up to the house of a top exec for a midnight rendezvous? She's right, Guy, it's not what you think. She's just selling cookies.

Dawn   What have you done?

Buddy   Oh, stop – stop with the fucking stupid questions. What do you think he's done? He's taken me hostage, he's beaten me, he's tortured me, and – honey? I think you're next.

Dawn   Guy, this is insane. Just put the gun down and let's talk about this.

Buddy   What the fuck do you think we've been doing all night? I don't think you fully appreciate the situation, dear. After you get past the 'Oops, he caught us' stage and realize we're both fucked, let me know, OK?

Dawn   Shut up, I've got nothing to do with you.

Buddy   Bullshit, Dawn, this is no time for lies. He's caught us.

Dawn   I never –

Buddy   What happened to standing by your man, Dawn? Oh, that's right. You don't stand by your men. You stand on them as you climb up to the next one's bed.

Dawn   Who the hell do you think you are?

Buddy   What are you doing here then?

Dawn   Why don't you guess what I'm doing?

Buddy   Come on, Dawn. Tell him about your life.

Dawn   What's that meant to –

Buddy   Your cheap little life.

Guy *raises the gun at* **Buddy**.

Guy   Shut up!

Dawn   Guy, you're acting like a child. You are no better than he is right now.

Guy   How long have you –

Dawn   I haven't –

Buddy   Yes! You can't trust her, Guy. I told you, for months.

Dawn   I promise.

Buddy   Good months, you know, if you add 'em up.

Dawn   Guy, it's not what you think.

Guy   Then why are you here?

Buddy   To work her fuckin' magic.

Dawn   No, Buddy. To tell you. It's over.

Buddy   What?

Dawn   It's over. I spoke to Daniel. Told him the truth.

Guy   Daniel?

Buddy   What do you mean, it's over?

Dawn   I mean that I'm sick, Buddy. That I'm sick of men with balls bigger than brains telling me what to do. That I've got to give action to get action. Because you know what? I'm through giving. And I'm through getting. And now, it's my time to take. Daniel's bringing *Afghani* back to me.

Guy   What?

Dawn   We're going with Stella.

Buddy   Bullshit.

Dawn   No. I'd never have let it go to you if I'd known you weren't President of Production. This is false pretenses.

Buddy   She's bluffing, Guy. Cyrus –

Dawn   Is going to hear the whole story first thing tomorrow morning. You're finished, Buddy. Come tomorrow, Stella's in charge and you're out on your ass.

Buddy   And where does that leave you?

Dawn   It's like you said, Buddy. I've been away from the big leagues for way too long.

Buddy   See? What did I tell you, Guy? She's the same as the rest.

Dawn   No, I'm not.

Buddy   No?

Dawn   No. I'm doing this with honor. Starting with *Afghani*. We're going to make it the way we wanted, before either of you two dipped your egos in the inkwell.

Guy   What?

Dawn   No changes.

Guy   But they're my changes.

Dawn   Not anymore, Guy. You're out.

Buddy   See?

Guy   What?

Buddy   She's screwing you, Guy.

Dawn   No. I'm saving you.

Guy   Saving me?

Dawn   You're free. You're out of this job, now. You can write. You can start again.

Guy   I don't want to start again.

Dawn   Well, now you don't have a choice.

Guy   No.

Dawn   Oh, come on, Guy. He was going to fire you anyway.

Buddy   Bullshit.

Dawn   Soon as the movie was made.

Guy   He can't fire me.

Buddy   That's right.

Guy   He needs me.

Dawn   Open your eyes. He was using you.

Buddy   No.

Dawn   Using you to get to me.

Buddy   She's stealing your film, Guy.

Dawn   My film.

Guy   But it's my rewrite, it –

Buddy   Made it better.

Dawn   No.

Buddy   Much better, Guy. I know it, you know it –

Dawn   Don't listen to him.

Buddy   Daniel fuckin' knows it.

Dawn   You're wrong, Buddy.

Buddy   Am I?

Dawn   Yes.

Buddy   'Cause all of a sudden you've changed Daniel's mind?

Dawn   Yes.

Buddy   With this crock of horseshit? Please. How do you think she really convinced him, Guy? In a single night? How d'you think she managed that, huh, logical fuckin' argument?

Dawn   I just told him the truth.

Buddy   You just talked, huh?

Dawn   Yes.

Buddy   You got a powerful mouth, Dawn, but that stretches my fuckin' imagination.

Dawn   Screw you.

Buddy   Right now? Honey, I'd say this was a bad time. I told you, Guy, she –

Guy *raises the gun above his head and fires.*

Guy   Shut up! Both of you, shut up!

Dawn   Put the gun down.

Guy   No.

Buddy   Come on, Guy.

Guy   You screwed me.

Buddy   She screwed you.

Dawn   Don't, Guy.

Buddy (*to* **Dawn**)   Leave him alone. (*To* **Guy**.) You know what you have to do, kid. You have no choice.

Dawn   Don't do this.

Buddy   You've got to take it.

Dawn   We can fix this.

Buddy   You don't take it I got no sympathy for you.

Dawn   You can start again.

Buddy   It's yours.

Dawn   You're good.

Buddy   She fucked me while you were making coffee.

Dawn   You're a good man.

Buddy   Be a man.

Dawn   Please, Guy.

Buddy   You need this.

Dawn   I love you.

Buddy   Will you stay the fuck out of this!

Dawn   I am trying to save your life.

Buddy   And I am trying to give Guy his. He can't fuck his way through the ranks nearly as well as you can, Dawn. He's got to kick and fight and scratch his way there. He doesn't have a choice. You have nothing to contribute to this, so stay the fuck out.

Beat.

Dawn   You know what? Go ahead. Shoot him. I don't care.

Buddy   Yabba dabba doo. All right, Guy. Let's finish this. Show me what you're made of. Show me what you've learned. Don't let me down, son. Everything I've taught you comes down to this. This is the only way that you can hope to survive. Look at my face. Look at your hands. They hurt. They bleed. Because life is not a movie. What do you want, Guy? Look at me. What do you want? Let's do this thing. Let's finish it.

Guy *lowers the gun.*

Guy   I'm sorry.

Beat. **Buddy** *chooses his moment and pounces.*

Buddy   Do it. Come on, do it now!

Guy *raises the gun. Blackout. A single shot is fired.*

Scene Seven

Keystone. **Guy** *stands behind his desk packing his things into a large box. The 'Buddy Ackerman' written on the closed doors of* **Buddy**'s *old office is half changed and now reads 'Guy Ackerman'. The windows of the office are frosted.* **Jack** *stands at the foot of* **Guy**'s *desk, watching him. Beat.*

Jack   This is unbelievable. You know that, right? Unbelievable.

Guy   Maybe.

Jack   No, I'm sorry. I know we're meant to be grievin' an' all, but sooner or later you got to face facts. Focus on the positive. You are one lucky bastard, Guy. With Buddy, you know, 'up above', you're going to be running this place.

Guy   So it would seem.

Jack   And you know what? I bet deep down everybody's relieved.

Guy   Not everybody, Jack.

Jack   Just no one's got the cojones to say it. And anyway, you deserve it.

Guy   Yeah. Maybe I do.

Beat.

Jack   So, you got any tips for me? Can't wait to get started, you know?

Guy   Yeah. Yeah, I do, Jack. (*Beat.*) Shut up, listen, and learn. Everybody's going to want to give you the same advice. Tell you to pay your dues. Ask you to do them a favor. Do this for us. They all want you to play by the rules, Jack. Their rules. Well, save that candy-striped crap for the Wall Street wimps. Because the only interests that you need to protect are yours. And the only needs that you have to serve are yours. So the only question that you really need to answer is this. And think about this, Jack. What do you really want?

Jack   OK.

Beat.

Guy   Well?

Jack   I don't know yet.

Guy   Neither did I.

Suddenly, the doors of **Buddy***'s old office sling open.* **Buddy** *stands in the doorway, supporting himself with a cane. His face is scarred.*

He ushers **Cyrus** *and* **Daniel** *out of the office. All of them are laughing.*

Cyrus   And you're sure Dakota's on board?

Buddy   After the gross on number one, she won't work with anyone else.

Daniel   What can I say? We have a rapport.

Cyrus   You got her an Oscar, you damn well should. So when do I see the script?

Buddy   Soon, I promise.

Cyrus   Wonderful. You can tell me all about it over lunch.

Buddy   Can't wait. I'll just finish up here, be with you in half an hour.

Cyrus (*to* **Daniel**)   He never stops. Come on, Dan. Let's eat.

Cyrus *and* **Daniel** *exit. Beat.* **Buddy** *turns to* **Guy**.

Buddy   Where's my rewrite on the *Arab* sequel? You said yesterday.

Guy   I said tomorrow.

Buddy   You said yesterday.

Beat.

Guy   Sorry.

Buddy   On my desk tonight.

Guy   I can't, I –

Buddy   What? You have a date?

Beat.

Guy   No. No, I don't.

Buddy   And it better be gold, Guy. I don't want to look inconsistent.

Jack *clears his throat.*

Guy   Buddy, this is Jack, my new assistant.

Buddy   'Jack'. I like that. It's functional.

Jack   It's an honour to meet you, Mr President.

Buddy   Oh, I appreciate the gesture, Jack, but you're lickin' the wrong boots. Your new boss here's the youngest exec we've ever had.

Jack   I know.

Buddy   Pure dedication.

Guy   No.

Buddy (*to* **Guy**)   Don't be so modest.

Jack   I been trying to tell him. I mean, a jilted lover holds you hostage, beats you, tortures you, and he rides in and saves the day. It's unbelievable.

Buddy   You'd think.

Guy   That's not quite how it happened, Jack.

Jack   That's not quite the way it happened? Shit. Give him a wifebeater, he's John McClane.

Guy   I was delivering some scripts and I happened to be there.

Jack   You shot her, man. You're a real hero. I tell you, I'd love an excuse like that to pull a gun on some of my exes.

Buddy   Well, Jack, stick with Guy here and you might just get the chance. Now quick, people, I need coffee. I've got to be at the club in twenty minutes.

Guy   Jack, would you mind?

Buddy   No, no, Jack, don't you trouble yourself. Smart as you are, I don't think I'll ever find anyone who can make my coffee quite as well as Guy does. (*To* **Guy**.) Upstairs. Two minutes.

Beat.

Guy   Yes, sir.

Buddy (*to* **Jack**)   You, follow me. Matthew's things aren't gonna trash themselves.

Jack (*standing*)   Whatever you say, Mr President.

Buddy   God, I love this job. Oh, and – Guy? One other thing. I need a restaurant. Nine o'clock tonight. Two people.

Guy   The club?

Buddy   No. Somewhere romantic.

Guy   Romantic?

Buddy   Yeah. My ex-wife's in town.

Beat. **Buddy** *smiles. He looks to* **Jack**.

Buddy   What is it about the good ones, Jack? You screw 'em over to the end of the earth, but they see you in pain and suddenly all those grudges, all that pride, it just melts away. Just like in a movie. Maybe I'm getting old, but I tell you, it'd take one hell of a dream to make me pass up a girl like that. (*Beat. To* **Guy**.) So, uh, someplace special, huh? I'm sure you know the type.

Beat.

Guy   Yeah. I do.

Buddy   That's my Guy. (*Beat.*) Look at him, Jack. Solid gold success. How's that sound to you?

Jack   Sounds good, Mr Ackerman.

Buddy   I bet it does, Jack. I'd bet my life on it.

Buddy *leaves.* **Jack** *smiles elatedly at* **Guy** *and scurries out.*

Guy *looks around him. The phone starts to ring. He picks up a windup toy off his desk, winds it up, and sets it loose. He lets the phone carry on ringing and watches the windup toy play out its little journey. The noise of the windup toy increases, blending with the phone noise and together building to a crescendo, at which the windup toy plummets to the floor.*

Blackout and silence.